Marie°

Nice to have made
your acquaintence at the
workshop. May you become a
linguist in the New Language of
Work.

Best Regards, Joseph

Best Regards, [signature] 6/22/96

THE NEW LANGUAGE OF WORK

Danny G. Langdon

HRD PRESS, INC.
AMHERST, MASSACHUSETTS

Published by Human Resources Development Press, Inc.
22 Amherst Road
Amherst, Massachusetts 01002
1-800-822-2801

ISBN 0-87425-990-8

Production Services by Page Design Services
Editorial Services by Mary George
Cover Design by Old Mill Graphics

CONTENTS

FIGURES

ACKNOWLEDGMENTS

I would like to extend my gratitude to the many people who have helped me so much over the years, generously sharing their ideas and influencing my work in positive ways. I sincerely wish I could recognize and give credit to each and every person who has contributed in some way to this volume. Let me assure you that any omissions are unintentional.

Through professional associations and forums, I have come into contact with a wealth of fine individuals whose presentations on their own work have had an impact on mine. Many thanks to Bill Deterline, Geary Rummler, Don Tosti, Kathleen Whiteside, Dick Lincoln, Claude Lineberry, Bob Mager, Bob Horn, Bob Powers, Joe Harless, George Geis, Dick Mentzer, Jay Alden, Judy Springer, Susan Markle, Don Bullock, Tom Gilbert, Roger Addison, Margo Murray, Ruth Ashley, Stephanie Jackson, Ivan Horabin, Sivasialam Thiagarajan, Fred Wells, Gabe Ofiesh, Kathryn Keeler, James Russell, Philip Tiemann, Erica Keeps, Harold Stolovitch, Gene Meyers, Karl-Heinz Fletsig, and Roger Kaufman. I would also like to thank the numerous authors with whom I worked as series editor on the 40-volume Instructional Design Library. What a treasure chest of people to know! Their writing and our conversations have come to mind often during my work on this volume, lending me invaluable assistance.

It is important to recognize that the Language of Work is imbedded in the principles and techniques of a Human Performance Technology approach to improving individual, team, and organization performance. The National Society for Performance and Instruction (NSPI), headquarters in Washington, D.C., is the prime advocacy group of professionals who use this particular technological approach to improving human performance in business, government, and education. As a past international president and attendee at 25 conferences, I have had the great pleasure to give and receive intellectually with this group. Many of the early founders and practitioners of NSPI are responsible for originally defining models of human behavior based, in varying ways, on inputs, conditions, process, outputs, consequences, feedback, and the like— even though they may have used other words to label the six basic elements of the language of work. I wish to acknowledge in particular the work of Ludwig Von Bertalanffy, Dr. B.F. Skinner, Tom Gilbert, Joe Harless, Lloyd E. Homme, Donald Tosti, William A. Deterline, and Roger A. Kaufman.

There is a group of individuals who provided some insightful response survey data that was used to confirm the concepts presented in this book. I would like to thank the following for their perspective: Charles Mannell, Xilinx, Turan Ceran, DMJM, Ralph Goldsworthy, International Rectifier, James Kennedy, Teledyne Electronic Systems, Jim Nelson, Teradyne, Timothy Slipp, Nelco, Robert Jackson, Beckman, and Bijan Anvar, Northrop.

I am especially indebted to those individuals who were directly involved in the writing of this book, including:

- Scott Nelson, chief executive officer of First Security Bank; Mel D'Souza, business unit manager of Engineering Services, ITC Corporation, San Bernardino, California, office; and the professional engineering staff of the San Bernardino office.

- Gene J. Myers, my friend and colleague, who provided me with many useful suggestions.

- Chris Hunter, of HRD Press, who guided the progress of the final draft. He made me realize what being a good publisher is all about.

- Mary George, of HRD Press, who made me reconsider content, do major chapter revisions, and look again at my whole approach. More than anything else, she made sure that the Language of Work was understandable in the language of English.

I am indebted as well to my mother, Marian O. Langdon. As a quintessential professional woman and loving mother, she taught me analytical techniques in the context of caring for others.

I am most indebted, however, to my wife and colleague in life and business, Kathleen Whiteside Langdon. She edited, contributed ideas, and made me rethink how I was attempting to communicate my thoughts. She loves me, as I passionately love her, and for her concern and support in life I am deeply grateful. She is, as I so proudly tell others, both inside and out the beautiful Kathleen.

ABOUT THE AUTHOR

Danny G. Langdon is the originator and leading exponent of the Language of Work approach to business improvement. Mr. Langdon is the president of Performance International in Santa Monica, CA, (310-453-8440), a training and consulting firm that brings managers and workers together in the management development effort. A past international president of the National Society for Performance and Instruction, he has spoken at the White House, administered major training and quality improvement efforts in leading Fortune 500 companies, and provided consulting services to various businesses. He has served as an adjunct faculty member of The American College, University of Southern California, and Boise State University. Mr. Langdon believes in training and developing managers and workers together because his experience has taught him that the shift to high-performing businesses requires a corresponding paradigm shift in management development, one that includes, rather than excludes, the affected workers. For his efforts, he has won major awards in outstanding new systematic processes and innovative human performance aids.

INTRODUCTION

Unless everyone understands what a work process is, how to map it, how to analyze and quantify its essential elements, no organization will be able to reap the enormous gains in performance that come with an involved and empowered work force.

> – Frank Doyle, Executive Vice President, General Electric
> Quoted in *Al Gore Report on Reinventing Government*

As businesspeople, most of us have learned from our own experience how poor communication impedes the successful execution, administration, implementation, measurement, and improvement of work. Employees struggle with role clarification, uncertain where they stand in relation to others in the organization; managers give inadequate task assignments and performance reviews, not really knowing how the business works; attempts to improve the organization fail because employees and managers do not understand each other, nor the organization's policies and procedures. Although we have been able to establish certain lines of communication that, in the long run, do hold us together, we know there is something missing—some vital connection that will help us improve our organizations rather than merely ensure their survival.

This book is designed to help us make that connection—to fill the fundamental communication gap that affects everyone who works in business, from employees to managers to executives. The major source of the problem is not difficult to diagnose: We lack a basic, complete work language that provides us with a clear definition of work and a common method of communicating. Solving this problem, however, is not easy. It demands a preliminary understanding of language itself and an analysis of the business organization as a world, or "sphere," whose members have specific communications needs that correspond to their roles in this sphere. Ultimately, it calls for *a new language of work,* a model of communication that not only unifies the various components of the organization in a general way, but fulfills the specific needs of those who bring those components to life: the workers and the managers.

The purpose of this book, therefore, is threefold:

1. To provide a common language of work so that clear lines of communication can be established between workers and managers (including executives), and among the members of these two basic groups. This work language will be known simply as the Language of Work.

2. To shape the common language into a model, or paradigm, of work
   that everyone can use to help meet workplace demands such as:

   - Identifying work needs
   - Solving work problems
   - Measuring work
   - Improving performance
   - Specifying necessary changes
   - Assigning, executing, and administering work
   - Analyzing work

3. To demonstrate the many practical work application tools that you, whether
   as a manager or a worker, can use in conjunction with this language to meet
   your daily work needs.

Introducing a new language of work into an organization is quite a formidable goal—and the results are a great deal to hope for—but this goal *can be achieved,* and the results *are attainable.* Having personally used this system in business, I know that the concepts in this book really do work. Businesses that use continuous improvement (i.e., total quality management) will find these concepts particularly useful, although it is important to stress that the concepts are applicable to any business, work group, or individual. In all cases, the "Language of Work" (the term I shall use to specify our new language) actually threatens to close that troublesome communication gap once and for all.

LEARNING THE LANGUAGE OF WORK

As learning to apply any new system ultimately begins with the individual learner, *The New Language of Work* initially focuses on you, whether you are a worker, a manager, or an executive. Chapters 1 and 2, along with this introduction, will help you build the theoretical foundation you need in order to apply the work language on a practical level. Then, in Chapter 3, we will see how you as an individual can indeed use this work language to improve your communication skills. Once you have learned to apply this language to your own job needs and various work functions (such as problem solving and work measurement), your learning base will broaden to include other major areas of the organization. In Chapters 4 through 6, we will see the positive effects the work language can have on your work group, your relationship with other work groups, the process you and others use to produce work, and the business organization as a whole — which we will refer to in this book as the Business Sphere. Finally, in Chapter 7, you will learn how the Language of Work can be introduced into the Business Sphere.

Learning the new work language may at times seem a repetitive process, yet repetition is key to learning any new language. If at first the vocabulary seems foreign to you, remember that understanding and using these words will quickly become second nature to you as your definition of work expands and you learn how to apply the Language of Work to your many job functions. Then, as you use common work language with others, especially in manager/worker relationships, it will virtually become an intuitive way of thinking and acting. You will see how this language can be used by everyone in the work force to communicate with one another and thus comprehend what the business they work in is all about. Its value will appear in many ways: as workers and managers do their work more effectively and efficiently; as teams build teamwork and clarify team roles; as work groups and processes are analyzed, measured, and improved; as even the entire business unit is analyzed, measured, and improved. Moreover, you will see how the Language of Work helps to bind and move the business together in ways never before possible.

TECHNICAL LANGUAGES AND FINANCIAL LANGUAGE

It is important to understand that the Language of Work is quite different from the kind of "language" whose terminology is particular to one area of work. As there are many areas of work, there are many languages of this type. In the context of the business world, these various methods of communication can be categorized under two general headings: technical language and financial language.

Technical language provides us with a vocabulary for precisely describing the practical aspects of work: what we do in our particular skill area, what tools help us do it, and what knowledge we must draw on to do it well. For example, in explaining a job, an engineer may use words like *critical path, failure analysis,* or *tensile strength,* while a trainer may use *needs assessment, validation,* or *visualization,* and an accountant, *receivables, depreciation,* or *amortization.* The more complex the job, the more technical the terminology, and the harder it is for workers and managers from other areas of the organization to understand what that job entails and how to refer to it when attempting to improve performance in the workplace. Moreover, communication problems between workers who speak the same technical language are not rare, so it is not surprising that at times even their own managers may not grasp what they are talking about. Technical language simply does not lend itself to universal application. It is important, but it does not fundamentally help hands-on workers and their managers come together and communicate clearly about work and how to improve it.

Financial language is used mainly by executives and managers, although it is not necessarily foreign to workers. Its vocabulary includes words such as *profit, loss,* P/E *ratio,* and even terms like *mission, objectives,* and *strategies.* It is an important business language because it helps management draw up and implement work plans, set the standards needed for the organization's survival, and establish ways to communicate with stockholders and stakeholders so that the organization will grow. But this is the language of the few, not the many. Although workers may occasionally refer to an organization's profit or loss and somewhat understand its implications for them, financial language does not provide a vocabulary for defining the workers' jobs and conveying how to improve job performance. Telling the work force that profit must be improved does not tell them how to improve profits. Neither does this language really facilitate communication about the administration and execution of work even though organizations often depend on it to function in this way. Consequently, the communication gap just widens.

The limitations of technical language and financial language throw into relief the essential feature of the Language of Work: its universality. It is a *common work language*—a fundamental means of communication that workers and managers can use to understand one another better and to make their work more effective and efficient. How widespread is the need for this common work language? Thirty years of experience in developing performance improvement programs has led me to believe the need is quite widespread indeed. Is its absence a problem that affects you personally? Could your own communication skills be improved? The Work Communications Survey provided at the conclusion of this introduction will help you determine the answers.

WORKERS AND MANAGERS

Throughout this book, for the sake of clarity and easy reference, I have divided the work force into two broad categories: workers and managers. *Workers* include any individual or team that is nonadministrative in nature; thus, most people in a business are workers. *Managers* include those who supervise workers. Ideally, managers facilitate job performance; that is, they provide the means for work, aid in the utilization of it, and provide reinforcement for work completed. Supervisors at any level of management, including the executive level, are placed in this category.

Of course, managers are workers too. However, for our purposes here, we need to distinguish between those who supervise and those who receive supervision. I have found that using the terms *workers* and *managers* is the simplest way to do this. Where it is necessary to make further distinctions and provide more detail, I have done so; for example, the needs of executive management are addressed separately.

THE EXAMPLES USED IN THIS BOOK

The following hypothetical business and three representative jobs will be used throughout this book to illustrate the application of the Language of Work to various business communication needs.

The Engineering Company

Our sample business, an engineering company, specializes in providing design, remediation (clean-up), project management, and other services, as well as a few products, for meeting the needs of various businesses and government agencies in the environmental field. Because the company is in the environmental services business, it must pay particular attention to government regulations and public concern.

The business employs a variety of workers and managers. Most of its professional work force is comprised of engineers, with some geologists and a variety of technical specialists in human resources, proposal development, marketing and sales, project management, health and safety, quality, accounting, office management, and the like.

The Workers

1. CAD Engineer—John

John is an engineer whose current specialty is the use of a computer-aided design (CAD) system to produce engineering drawings. This means he collects data from the field by himself or with others, reviews inspection reports, determines the cost of materials and services, and under the direction of his lead manager and within health and safety guidelines, designs drawings that meet specific needs. At times John must provide information to the next position in line—the proposal writer—in the form of technical data, budgets, and procedures, all of which will be used to write proposals to potential clients. Although part of the Engineering department, John occasionally works on the actual execution of a project, joining a project team that utilizes a project management approach to execute the work. John would like to be a project manager in the near future.

2. Proposal Writer — Lee

Lee is a proposal writer who is part of the Proposal Development department. His job is to write proposals and related cost considerations in response to client requests for services from the engineering company. Typically this involves working with engineers, managers, salespeople, and training personnel to collect data, write capability statements, determine the technologies that will be used, set up project schedules, and create overall plans for meeting client needs. Lee writes these specifications into a proposal and corresponding cost proposal. Management reviews all the information for accuracy and completeness. If the proposal is initially accepted by the client along with ones written by other companies, Lee may also have to work with a group of engineers and other workers, who will prepare and give an oral presentation to the potential client. In this way, the client can personally meet the proposed project team and ask questions before deciding whether to award a contract to the engineering company or to its competition.

3. Trainer — Monica

Monica is a professional trainer who is part of the Human Resources department. She uses a highly systematic approach to the design, development, and implementation of training needs as defined by the engineering company. This approach is called

Instructional Technology. The courses and materials Monica develops are in a variety of forms, from lecture to computer-aided instruction. She works with a number of individuals and teams, particularly engineers, who serve as content experts, and proposal writers, who use her assistance to develop and practice oral presentations.

Each of these three job positions gives us a different perspective on the Language of Work. As samples, they were designed to facilitate an understanding of how this common work language can be applied to *any job*. The engineering position was chosen because it is highly technical. As most of us are unfamiliar with the job of a proposal writer, this position was selected to illustrate how the work language can greatly aid our understanding and appreciation of jobs about which we know little or nothing but should know something. The trainer position represents a job with which many of us are familiar, and it is a useful reference when discussing role relationships, teams, and the like.

WORK COMMUNICATIONS SURVEY

How well does your company communicate the fundamental aspects of administering work and getting it completed? How clear are job descriptions and the definitions of team roles? Are work assignments well defined? The following Work Communications Survey will help you answer these and many other important questions about the current level of communication in your company.

When completing this survey, be honest about the quality of communication in your company. Review the results to get a comprehensive picture of what is really going on in your business. Then prepare yourself for learning a new way to meet the communication challenges of the workplace. I hope you find the Language of Work as rewarding as I have, and that your workplace enjoys the positive results I have witnessed in so many businesses.

WORK COMMUNICATIONS SURVEY

Assess the quality of communication in your company regarding the following aspects of work.

	Very Satisfactory	Satisfactory	Minimal	Lacking
1. Performance review	❏	❏	❏	❏
2. Receiving feedback while a task is worked on	❏	❏	❏	❏
3. Work assignments	❏	❏	❏	❏
4. Guidance as a task is being worked on	❏	❏	❏	❏
5. Following policies and procedures	❏	❏	❏	❏
6. Knowing company policies and procedures	❏	❏	❏	❏
7. Expressing ideas to others about work in progress	❏	❏	❏	❏
8. Communicating a suggested change in procedure	❏	❏	❏	❏
9. Knowing how to measure, identify, and accurately define a needed change	❏	❏	❏	❏
10. Knowing standards to be achieved	❏	❏	❏	❏
11. Evaluating satisfaction of an internal or external client	❏	❏	❏	❏
12. Following through with a client	❏	❏	❏	❏
13. Defining and executing career development	❏	❏	❏	❏
14. Management's follow-up to providing for your needs	❏	❏	❏	❏
15. Giving proper reinforcement for completed tasks to others	❏	❏	❏	❏

	Very Satisfactory	Satisfactory	Minimal	Lacking
16. Identification of worker needs	❏	❏	❏	❏
17. Doing strategic planning and actually following through	❏	❏	❏	❏
18. Communicating work results to workers	❏	❏	❏	❏
19. Solving problems with others	❏	❏	❏	❏
20. Measuring work accurately	❏	❏	❏	❏
21. Knowing and being able to explain to others how our business works from beginning to end	❏	❏	❏	❏
22. Measuring and improving my own job	❏	❏	❏	❏
23. Measuring and improving my work group	❏	❏	❏	❏
24. Improving relations with other work groups	❏	❏	❏	❏
25. Getting my output to others on time	❏	❏	❏	❏
26. Definition of team roles	❏	❏	❏	❏
27. Measuring team success	❏	❏	❏	❏
28. Improving quality	❏	❏	❏	❏
29. Job description	❏	❏	❏	❏
30. Selection of new workers and managers	❏	❏	❏	❏
31. Work planning	❏	❏	❏	❏

CHAPTER 1

A COMMON LANGUAGE OF WORK

To establish a common work language that everyone, workers and managers alike, can use to increase communication and successfully address the needs of the workplace, it is first necessary to understand what we mean by the term *language*. According to *Merriam-Webster's Collegiate Dictionary,* the definition of language is "the words, their pronunciation, and the methods of combining them used and understood by a community." To carry this definition one step further, we can say that a language must include four essential elements:

- Words that carry specific meaning

- Syntax—a logical system of ordering the words so that they convey meaning in relation to one another

- Message—the meaning you want to convey. A message may contain an idea, a fact, a direction, or similar content

- A means of transmission (medium)—that which can be used to transmit or apply the message

Clear and complete communication depends upon the presence of these elements; they are intrinsic to language (i.e., language cannot exist without them). However, their proper use is contingent upon the user. For example, someone who has a limited vocabulary may not be able to convey a message in the most precise terms. Therefore, if we are to construct a common work language, we must ensure that everyone is familiar with the same vocabulary.

To understand the importance of syntax, first consider the meaning of the following eight words:

to	have
and	words
must	language
syntax	communicate

Now, here are two combinations among the many possible combinations of these eight words:

- Language words must to have and communicate syntax

- Communicate have and to syntax must language words

Do either of these combinations make sense to you? Because you are familiar with the individual words and their definitions, some meaning is conveyed; but both a proper word order and an understandable message are missing. We must use some conventional system, or syntax, to communicate clearly.

Simply ordering words so that they form a structurally coherent sentence is not enough, however. We must also make sure the words and their order correspond to the meaning we want to communicate. It is quite possible, for instance, that after reading the above word combinations, you were able to rearrange the words and make a fairly coherent sentence, as if solving a puzzle. But would this necessarily mean you had produced a sentence with a logical meaning or had discovered my intended message? Perhaps you came up with the following:

- Syntax must have words and language to communicate.

- Words must have syntax and language to communicate.

Although these combinations are structurally coherent—intelligible enough to convey an idea—neither sentence has a completely logical meaning; therefore it would be reasonable to conclude that you must continue to work on the "puzzle" to determine the message.

Although these two sentences do not convey the message that I had in mind, their structural coherence is a useful illustration of one of the most fundamental patterns of syntax: subject-verb-object. Anyone who has learned English as a second language or who has received traditional instruction in English grammar is likely to be familiar with this basic pattern, which both sentences clearly fit. For example: Syntax (*subject*) must have (*verb*) words (*object*) and language (*object*) to communicate. (The phrase *to communicate* is an infinitive that tells us why "syntax must have words and language.") The problem with either sentence is that, as the eight words above were rearranged to form a coherent structure, the true subject was mistaken for an object. To put it simply, two pieces of the puzzle were misplaced. When the words are ordered correctly, we finally produce a sentence whose meaning corresponds to the intended message:

Language	**must have**	**words and syntax**	**to communicate.**
subject	*verb*	*objects*	

This combination of the eight words communicates because it has *defined words* and *syntax* properly used to convey a *message* through the *medium* of the written word. It is a message of primary significance for the construction of the Language of Work.

A LANGUAGE HAS

• DEFINED WORDS
• SYNTAX
• MESSAGE
• A MEANS OF TRANSMISSION (MEDIUM)

We cannot build a useful work language if the four requirements above are not met. The work language presented in this book fulfills each requirement through the following four features:

A LANGUAGE HAS	THE LANGUAGE OF WORK HAS
• DEFINED WORDS	• A LEXICON OF SIX DEFINED WORDS
• SYNTAX	• THE PERFORMANCE PARADIGM
• MESSAGE	• WORK APPLICATIONS
• MEDIUM	• WORK APPLICATION TOOLS

In the remainder of this chapter, we will look more closely at these four features that support the status of the Language of Work as a language.

THE LEXICON OF THE LANGUAGE OF WORK

The lexicon of the Language of Work is composed of the following six words:

- Inputs
- Outputs
- Conditions
- Consequences
- Process
- Feedback

While this lexicon is brief, it is nonetheless powerful, as you will soon discover. Figure 1.1 provides a profile for each word, including its definition, its typical source in the workplace, and an example of its use. In the upcoming pages, each will be discussed separately, then in relation to the other three features of the Language of

THE LEXICON OF THE LANGUAGE OF WORK
The Six Elements of Work

ELEMENT	TYPICAL SOURCES	DEFINITION	EXAMPLE*
Inputs	• People • Ideas • Equipment • Facilities • Funds • Information • Specific requests	The resources and requests available or needed to produce outputs. What must be present for something (the output) to happen.	Talking to others to fully review someone's job performance.
Conditions	• Rules • Policies • Environment • Attitudes	Existing factors that influence the use of inputs and processes used to produce an output.	Following existing policy and a schedule for performance reviews.
Process	• Designing • Selling • Manufacturing • Servicing • Testing	The actions necessary for using the inputs to produce outputs, performed by someone or something under certain conditions.	A manager and worker sit down and discuss past and future job performance of the worker.
Outputs	• Services • Products • Facts • Knowledge	That which is produced as a result (product/service/knowledge) of using inputs under certain conditions and through a process.	The output of a performance review is a document (form).
Consequences	• Customer Satisfaction • Needs met • Problem solved • Opportunity realized	The effects that an output has on a person, product, service, or situation.	Includes worker and manager's understanding of what has occurred in the past and what will be done in the future. Another consequence is that they both feel better.
Feedback	• Client reactions • Information needs • Reinforcements	That which completes the work cycle; response to outputs that confirms success or indicates adjustment is needed. Also, response to processing.	Typical feedback on a performance plan might be that it could be improved in some way or that it does meet the individual's needs.

* The example is a performance review/appraisal between a manager and worker. In a collaborative effort, the manager and worker look at the previous performance of the worker and assess how well the worker did his or her job and what needs to be improved. They also look at career development opportunities.

Figure 1.1

Work: the Performance Paradigm, work applications, and work application tools. But first, to prepare for this material, it is helpful to analyze the kind of work you are performing right now: the reading of this book.

Understanding the Six-Word Lexicon: A Preliminary Analysis

Consider for a moment why you are reading this book and what you hope to gain from it. Are you seeking knowledge? Do you want some basic facts on which you can expand your thinking? Are you expecting tangible results? Do you want to learn some practical procedures for improving a business or your effectiveness as a manager?

It is more than likely that you hope to gain all of the above, which can be classified as *outputs*. They represent what you will "take away" from this book. The major *input* that makes it possible to achieve these outputs is the book itself, along with the individual inputs of the printed pages, diagrams, and other displays that make up the book. Inputs do not immediately lead to outputs, though; you must use a *process*.

In this case, what *process* do you use? I could complicate the answer by delineating all the steps of the process—the encoding and decoding that turns black squiggles on a white page into an understanding of what they mean. But for our purposes here, and for simplicity's sake, it is sufficient to capture the process in a single word: reading.

The process of reading links inputs and outputs, making it possible to achieve those outputs. However, the success of this process (or any other process) is subject to certain *conditions*. These conditions also have a direct influence on your use of the inputs. For example, the conditions of the room lighting and type size have an effect on your reading ability (the process), influencing how well you are able to use the book (the input) to acquire knowledge, facts, and so forth (the outputs). We usually have limited control over conditions. In the case of reading, you may be able to control room lighting, improving it if necessary, but you cannot change the physical state of the book itself, for example, its type size or print clarity.

What will result from your achieving the outputs? There is a range of possibilities: you may feel good about the difference your new knowledge (output) has made in your job performance; you may be more motivated on the job; you may even feel enlightened. Results such as these are termed *consequences*. They appear similar to outputs but are really the results of outputs. For instance, a business profit is a consequence of producing various outputs, rather than an output itself. Feelings that result from outputs, such as client satisfaction, are also consequences. You will find it easier to identify outputs and consequences if you remember their primary distinction: Outputs are tangible things you get or produce, whereas consequences are the follow-up results of producing the output. This distinction affects how we deal with each of them in business, which we will explore later.

Finally, it is possible that you will receive *feedback* on the knowledge (output) you gained from this book. You may discuss with a colleague a procedure you learned and obtain an opinion on how well it might work or, if the colleague has read the book too, on how well you achieved the output. Feedback can result in revisions to process and output, and help to change conditions and consequences. For example, when certain people read this book prior to its publication and gave me constructive criticism (feedback) on it, I revised the book, incorporating their ideas (feedback) into the writing (process).

In short, you start with *inputs,* under certain *conditions,* and use a *process* (or *processes*) to arrive at *outputs,* which in turn result in *consequences* and lead you to seek or provide *feedback*.

Six-Word Lexicon	**Book-Reading Examples**
• Inputs:	Words, visuals, your needs
• Conditions:	Room lighting, type size
• Process:	Reading
• Outputs:	Knowledge, facts
• Consequences:	Satisfaction, practical application
• Feedback:	Reactions, comments to or from others

Remember that reading is not only the process but also the form of work we have just analyzed and that the six-word lexicon is applicable to any type of work.

In business, everything you do, everything a team does, everything an organization does, and every factor that is instrumental to achieving results—whether those results be a product, decision, or service—can be described and diagrammed using the six-word lexicon of the Language of Work. To understand how this is possible, we must turn to a more detailed explanation of each word, set within the context of a typical business organization. (For easy reference to these terms and their definitions, see Figure 1.1.)

The Six-Word Lexicon: Definitions and Details

1. Outputs — *That which is produced as a result (product/service/knowledge) of using inputs under certain conditions and through a process.*

Although outputs follow inputs, conditions, and process in the actual order of events in the workplace, the word *outputs* is given first position in this section to emphasize a fundamental prerequisite of successful work performance: determining and defining the particular outputs we want to achieve. This is of first and foremost importance, for we must understand where we are supposed to be heading as individuals, work groups, business units, and in the use of processes. Outputs are not blind results; they are the results of achieving the goals we have set. As fundamental as they are, outputs can only be achieved if well defined and attended to.

The following transportation analogy points out the significance of defining our outputs before engaging in *any* other aspect of work. Suppose you know that you must travel somewhere, but instead of first finding out what the destination is, you decide what mode of transportation you will use to get there. You select your favorite type of car, buy it, and later feel quite satisfied with your purchase as you drive through Los Angeles, the city in which you live. Then you are told that your destination (goal) is Australia. However much you like the car (your process), you suddenly wish it were a boat or a plane; however long you look at it, hoping to transform it into a mode of transportation that can get you across the Pacific Ocean, it remains a car—and worthless for achieving your goal. The problem: You did not DEFINE AUSTRALIA FIRST; that is, you decided how you were going to meet the goal before you knew the precise details and requirements of the goal. The lesson: Always fully define outputs (work goals) before acting on achieving them. Whenever you see the statement DEFINE AUSTRALIA FIRST in this book, it means we need to define our outputs before we define any other element of work.

To set this problem in the context of business, ask yourself these questions: How often have you seen a manager tell workers what to do before describing what the end product (output) should look like? Or how often has a manger failed to specify what standards are to be met before describing the procedure necessary for meeting them? In either case, what the manager has done is similar to telling someone to fly an airplane but not divulging where it is to be landed or specifying how much fuel the plane will need to reach its destination. It's no wonder that workers "crash land" their work on occasion. They are not given the information they need to form a complete picture of work and to understand the order, or syntax, of the elements that compose work.

Problems in this area tend to be rooted in a limited view of what defines work, as when a manager says, "We're in business to *do work!*" Actually, *doing work* is a process, not a result. What the manager really wants to say is that the results of work (*outputs*) are important. We are not in business to do work but to produce outputs. Businesses are in business to produce outputs. Those that emphasize doing work spend far more time doing work than getting the product or service out; those that emphasize getting the product out, such as quality-driven businesses, do so at a more cost-effective and efficient level. The more you apply the Language of Work to business, the more you will come to understand how such a shift in emphasis can have profound effects on an organization's measure of success and how critical it is to verbalize and act on all six elements of work.

Examples of output generally fall into three categories: products, service, and knowledge. A widget is a product, advice is a service, and a fact learned is knowledge. A less obvious example of an output would be something like a performance review—the formal periodic assessment of worker and manager work. Some may think the discussion between the manager and the worker constitutes an output, but the discussion is the process they use to arrive at the output (an assessment or plan of action that will be followed). Remember that the knowledge, new ways of doing things, and facts that result from your reading this book are also examples of outputs.

2. Inputs — *The resources and requests available or needed to produce outputs.*

Naturally, to produce outputs you need some sort of primary material—"raw material," so to speak. This is your input. Whether something is an input or an output is often relative; that is, its status as an input or output depends on the context in which you are viewing it and your individual relationship to it. Thus, what is an input to you may be an output to someone else. For example, the output produced by a worker is the input that a supervisor used to do a performance review. Or the data in a study (output) produced by one worker is used by another as the input to produce an engineering drawing (output). In the process of doing business there are often many chains of output/input in which an individual's or a work group's output is input for the next individual or group in line.

Undoubtedly, the most important inputs for a business are client needs; without them, the business has no purpose. Federal Express, for instance, would not be in business if there were no client needs (inputs) to get packages to a distant location in a hurry; people would simply use the basic services of the federal postal system, which itself would not be in the overnight-delivery business, as there would be no client need for it. It is equally important to understand that all individual workers and managers have clients—clients that we call internal clients. Therefore, everyone in business has client needs as one of, if not the most significant of, his or her inputs.

In addition to the above, typical examples of inputs include people, ideas, equipment, facilities, funds, information, and specific requests for outputs.

3. Conditions — *Existing factors that influence the use of inputs and processes used to produce outputs.*

All work is performed under certain conditions. Conditions are factors that influence how outputs are produced (the use of inputs and processes). For example, company policy on performance reviews is one of the conditions that influences when and how a manager conducts (produces) such a review (output). There are quite a number of specific and general conditions that prevail in business. Company policy and procedures, as well as government regulations, are the more specific kinds of conditions. The business environment is a general condition. Attitude could be considered a condition, as it influences inputs, process, outputs, consequences, and feedback. The effect on work of an attitude such as "a day's pay for a day's work" will be different from that of "I get paid for whatever I produce, so I'll only produce what I must to keep my job." If many people in the workplace share the same attitude, it would also be a general condition.

As conditions are sometimes confused with inputs, it is important to learn how to distinguish between them. Whereas conditions *influence* how work is done, inputs *are used* to produce work results (outputs). Conditions have three particular features that help us distinguish between them and inputs: First, conditions would exist even if the inputs vanished (although they might not be especially useful to us if this happens). Second, conditions influence not only the use of the inputs but also the process, outputs, consequences, and feedback; inputs, on the other hand, are used merely to produce the outputs. Third, conditions generally cannot be changed by workers and lower-level managers, even though these groups can influence change. The essential thing to remember is this: *You must be aware of conditions and apply them. Inputs you use.*

Conditions can be, and often are, ignored by individuals—which results in all sorts of problems, from minor annoyances to major catastrophes. For instance, disregarding a safety condition (a policy) can be dangerous, and ignoring company policy on annual performance reviews can affect employee morale. Why would a person neglect to observe conditions? There are numerous possibilities, such as forgetfulness, a lack of emphasis on the consequences by management, a careless attitude on the part of the individual, intentional disregard. From a work improvement standpoint, present conditions can be reinforced or changed and people provided with some incentive to observe them.

Note that if we want work performance to accord to certain standards, we must establish the conditions necessary for performance to meet those standards. Consequently, when there is a performance problem, we must look closely at conditions to determine whether they are contributing factors. Naturally, there will be times when we find it necessary to establish new conditions or enhance existing conditions so that improvements are possible.

4. Process — *The actions necessary for using the inputs to produce outputs, performed by someone or something under certain conditions.*

Process is the part of work that most of us recognize. It is what we ordinarily think of when we use the term *work*, although technically work comprises all six parts of the work language, not just the process. Thinking of work as a process-only endeavor is one of the several flaws in how we typically view work that this book is intended to correct.

Examples of processes include designing, selling, manufacturing, servicing, constructing, testing, and many other "ings." Later on in this book, the importance of using systematic processes as an added means of improving work will be explained and stressed.

5. Consequences — *Natural or desired results of producing an output and their effects on a person, product, service, or situation.*

Among the most desirable consequences of producing an output is client satisfaction. For most businesses, this consequence is essential to survival. Although it is not as crucial a result for businesses who are sole source providers, such as government agencies, it nonetheless remains desirable for public relations reasons—particularly in times of shrinking financial resources. Their clientele perceive them in a better light, and in the case of a government agency, people may more readily accept taxing themselves to continue the agency's service. Equally important is the knowledge that positive consequences make the work situation more pleasant for the worker and the client.

There are, of course, many other consequences we desire from work. Some are very general, others are very specific. Although some come naturally, most require planning and must be given continuous attention. As a rule, consequences cannot be left to chance or expected to happen on their own; they must be planned for, and attended to, in their proper relation to the other five elements of work. When attention flags, problems occur, as the federal postal service discovered when it failed to attend to delivery times. The output (getting a package delivered) consistently did not have the desired consequence (reaching its destination on time), thus opening the way for attentive services, like Federal Express, to step into the market and increase their market share. Subsequent changes in the federal postal service may have corrected the problem, yet how many clients were lost as a *negative consequence* of this inattention?

Because consequences are important for the success of the business, they are also important for the morale and success of the individuals and work groups within the business. Yet if the consequences of producing outputs are desirable to the business but not matched by *rewards* for the workers, motivational problems develop. High levels of performance can drop and job dissatisfaction set in. "Nobody ever tells me I'm doing a good job," a worker may complain. Eventually this problem will affect the quality of output and the entire business. Lack of motivation is often at the root of the failure to perform (given that processing skills have been acquired), and it is commonly a response to a lack of recognition for helping to produce good outputs with desirable consequences. Attending to consequences—to one aspect of work—therefore also includes attending to worker morale and job satisfaction.

For further examples of consequences, consider the possible results of your supervisor conducting a performance review with you. The results could be negative, positive, or neutral, and they could include (among many other possible results) your subsequent attitude, the opportunities you see for the future, the meeting of your individual needs, and the company retaining your services because you are satisfied.

6. Feedback — *That which completes the cycle of work; response that confirms the outputs have been completed successfully or that indicates the process needs adjustment. Also, response to the inputs, conditions, and processes during the course of producing outputs.*

Feedback is the final element in the cycle of work performance. In general, it is information provided in response to outputs and processes. Feedback lets us know if work has been done correctly or needs to be improved; it helps us judge the quality of an output *when the output is completed*. For example, you are receiving feedback when a customer complains about the quality of a service. Feedback also lets us know how work is proceeding during the course of producing an output; it helps us judge the quality of an output *before the output is completed*. When a manager asks a worker for information during a process to produce an output, the manager is asking for feedback. The manager can then use this feedback to adjust the process as needed.

The Language of Work helps us recognize the full potential of feedback as an element of work that can be used across the entire range of work performance. Presently, this element is often viewed, and therefore used, in a limited way. Consider the case of a worker receiving feedback during a performance review. It is likely that the feedback will focus on only one element of work—the worker's output—with little or no attention given to inputs, conditions, process, consequences, and feedback. When a performance review is conducted in this way, it is virtually inevitable that the review will overlook areas that have a bearing on a worker's performance, and this can have serious repercussions for work improvement.

Now compare the above to what happens when we apply the Language of Work to a performance review. Because our view of work includes *all* the elements of work, our understanding of feedback broadens and the focus of our review is more comprehensive. We may tell workers what changes are required in the use of the inputs they employ to produce the output, or in the conditions that affect the use of inputs and the process, output, and consequences. We can seek information from workers as they are engaged in the process of producing outputs and give them feedback on their performance of the process, indicating any changes that would improve either their performance or the process itself. Finally, we can, and should, tell workers how good the output is, indicating the level of client satisfaction (feedback on consequences). We can even ask when and where more or less feedback on any element of work would be useful. In essence, with the Language of Work, we can focus on, and provide feedback on, all the areas that are essential to performance improvement.

Remember: Feedback—a response to an input, a condition, a process, an output, or a consequence—fulfills information needs. It can be used to reveal weak areas of performance and equip workers with the knowledge they need to make adjustments to their performance. It lets us know whether the object of the feedback is satisfactory or not. If feedback from a person conducting a performance review indicates that a worker must greatly improve performance, then a low level of satisfaction is implied, if not directly stated. Feedback on satisfaction levels may also be quite direct, such as when a worker responds to a performance review by saying, "I found this review very useful." The person who conducted the review may in turn find the response (feedback) very useful.

THE PERFORMANCE PARADIGM—THE SYNTAX OF THE LANGUAGE OF WORK

The Language of Work grew out of a very analytical methodology for looking at the broader characteristics of human performance: Human Performance Technology (HPT). Among HPT's many concerns is how performance—or work, as one version of performance—may be accurately described. It offers several paradigms, or models, for performance description, one of which I have selected for the Language of Work because it functions particularly well for a variety of work applications. This paradigm is formally known as the Performance Paradigm, and it comprises the six-word lexicon to which you have already been introduced: inputs, conditions, process, outputs, consequences, and feedback. The Performance Paradigm fulfills the second major requirement of a language: syntax.

As the first section of this chapter illustrated, we need more than words if we are to communicate; we must have an ordering system for words—syntax—as well as a message and a means of transmission (medium). *Merriam-Webster's Collegiate Dictionary* provides us with the definition of syntax that is most appropriate for our use: "a connected or orderly system; harmonious arrangement of parts or elements." The Performance Paradigm, presented in Figure 1.2, clearly exhibits the "orderly system" of the Language of Work; it is the basic model for the syntax of our work language—a set of work performance words arranged in a meaningful relationship to one another. With these words and this paradigm, we can describe, diagram, explain, administer, measure, and improve work. To get an idea of how we might do this, let us turn to our sample business, the engineering company, and focus on John, the engineer.

Applying the Performance Paradigm

If we want to describe John's work, we can legitimately say, "John's work is to produce engineering drawings." The finished drawings are his output; they represent tangible products (or services). But if we end our description there, implying that John's work involves *only* the production of engineering drawings, we are not providing a complete description of his work. Unfortunately, meager work descriptions are legion in the world of business. All too often we encounter statements like the following, which are intended to serve as work descriptions but give us only a limited idea of work.

1. "I am responsible for producing X, Y, and Z."
2. "John is responsible for X, Y, and Z."
3. "Our strategic plan calls for producing 6 million Xs."
4. "I want you to produce 10 of those Xs."
5. "You did a good job last year making X, Y, and Zs. Keep it up!"

WORK SYNTAX: The Performance Paradigm

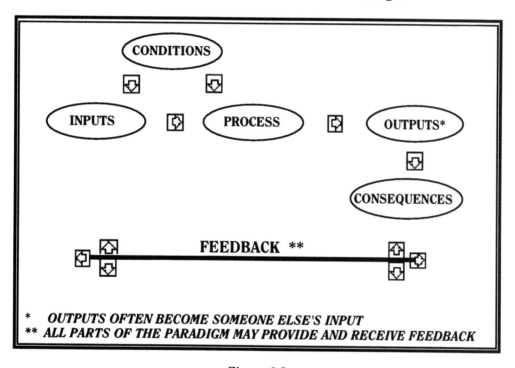

Figure 1.2

The first example is a statement by an individual worker. The next is a statement by a manager. The third is a statement by an executive. The fourth is from a manager telling a worker what to do. The fifth is an evaluation by a manager of a worker's performance over the past year. Are these complete statements of work? How often have you heard someone in the workplace supply only this much information as a directive or statement about your work? How often have you heard a manager assign or evaluate work with similar simple statements? The Performance Paradigm—the syntax of the new work language—offers a solution, expanding the meaning and description of work by executives, managers, and workers so that they can truly communicate more completely, effectively, and efficiently with one another. Figure 1.2

illustrates the dimensions of this expansion. Notice the order and relationship between the six elements of work and the model's comprehensive view of work. Now let us return to the description of John's work as an engineer to see what this means.

We already know that John produces an output: engineering drawings. To do this, John will need several pieces of input. He will certainly be given a client need as an input—someone requested the drawing! This could be an internal client who needs the drawing for a major project, or an external client with whom John is working directly. The client need is, therefore, one input. But John will also need other inputs, such as specifications of engineering data collected by himself or others, certain equipment (for example, a computer) to use to produce the drawing, funds, and the like. His work (in part) is really producing output with many forms of input. Consequently, the syntax we use in describing his work *must* include the fact that output is produced from inputs.

John's Work

But that is not all that makes up John's "work."

If we consult the Performance Paradigm, we see that John will need to follow a process in order to convert his inputs to an output. John trained as an engineer, and during that training he learned how to make drawings using a computer and what is known as a computer-aided design (CAD) system. CAD is therefore part of John's process for producing a drawing as an output. At this point, then, we know that John's work is composed of inputs, process, and output. Generally, these are three words that most managers and workers have heard and perhaps used, although not as everyday language in the workplace.

John's Work

But we still do not have a complete picture of John's work.

The Performance Paradigm reminds us there are a number of conditions that influence how John does what he does (the process) and what he uses (the inputs) to produce his output. For example, John works for an environmental engineering business. In making his drawings, he must observe the environmental regulations of the federal, state, and local government. There are also company policies and procedures that impose conditions on his work. So, John's work also involves being aware of, and conforming to, certain conditions.

John's Work

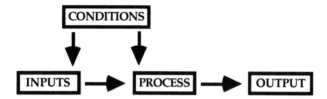

In the course of his work, John finds it helpful to make sure that he is doing work in the right way, so he checks with his manager and others about his work progress. As John's manager is a very conscientious supervisor, she often initiates the progress check and on occasion presents John with information that changes or enhances what he is doing. And, of course, when John has finished the drawing, his manager gives him feedback on how good the final product is and, if necessary, tells him what needs to be adjusted to make it just right for the current or next client. All of these interactions are designed to check, affirm, and learn *during* the process and *to confirm* when the output is completed. All are forms of feedback. Feedback, planned or requested, is a very important part of work. Thus, work now has five parts:

John's Work

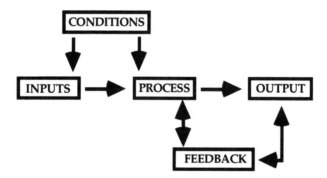

There is one final element of the Performance Paradigm that will complete the description of John's work: consequences. For example, the needs of John's client (internal or external) will have been met or not; an opportunity for John's success will have been realized or not. You will recall that consequences are not the output itself; rather, they are the natural or desired results of producing an output. All the elements of John's work have been accounted for according to the Performance Paradigm, and we now have a complete picture of John's work.

John's Work

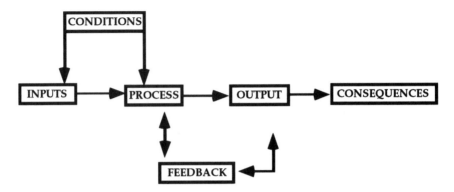

These six elements of the Performance Paradigm correspond, of course, to the six-word lexicon of the work language. The structure of the paradigm has several dimensions of meaning, including the following:

- Inputs are needed to produce outputs.

- Process links input and output.

- Conditions influence the use of input and the execution of process.

- Consequences result from the completion (or not) of output.

- Feedback is needed if inputs are to be used properly, process executed and adjusted to effective and efficient levels, conditions adhered to, output confirmed, and consequences reinforced.

- All six words are related, and a full description of work is *incomplete* without all six.

Thus far we have seen that the Language of Work has meaningful words and a syntax that connects the words in an orderly system, a harmonious arrangement of parts or elements. What remains is to learn how to apply the Language of Work so that it helps workers and managers do their work. In other words, the Language of Work needs to have messages to apply and a means through which to apply those messages.

Work Applications—The Messages Of The Language Of Work

The Language of Work can be applied to every performance need of a manager, worker, or team. We will refer to these various needs as *work applications*. They include all the necessary and usual activities we think of as job functions, accountabilities, responsibilities, and duties. In the Language of Work, work applications are the messages of the language.

Figure 1.3, the Manager's Work Applications Paradigm, lists the typical work applications of a manager (see next page). These applications include:

- Job description utilization

- Selecting workers

- Assigning work

- Facilitating the work of others

- Reinforcing work performance

- Measuring and improving quality

- Doing performance reviews

- Doing work needs assessment

- Planning work

- Analyzing work

The Language of Work will be applied to help execute, administer, measure, and evaluate the effectiveness and efficiency of the manager's work applications. These are the various *messages* that the manager is trying to communicate to workers and other managers in the organization. To the extent that workers and other managers in the organization "speak" (execute, administer, measure, and evaluate) the manager's same work language, the manager will find it easier to do his or her job. It is interesting to consider in this regard that typical management training and development has devoted its attention to training only the manager. It would be wise to train the manager and worker together in a common work language that would afford far greater understanding and cooperation in the applications of work. This will be one of the major goals and benefits to be realized through the use of the Language of Work.

There are also work applications that workers can use to apply the Language of Work. These are shown in Figure 1.4, Worker's Work Applications Paradigm.

They include:

- Job descriptions

- Role clarification

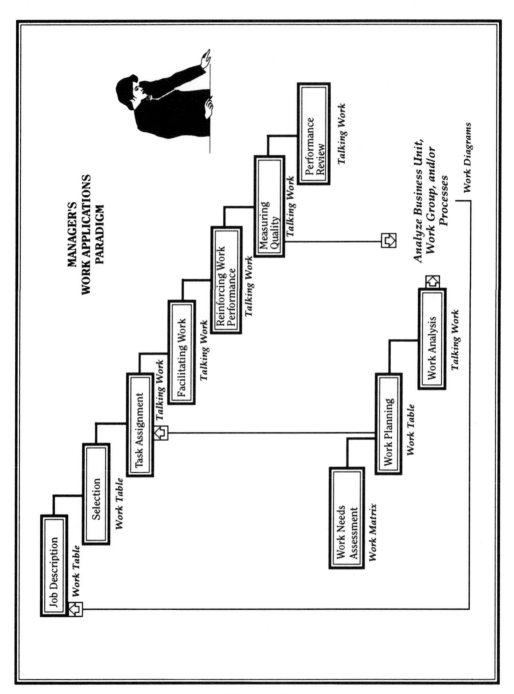

Figure 1.3

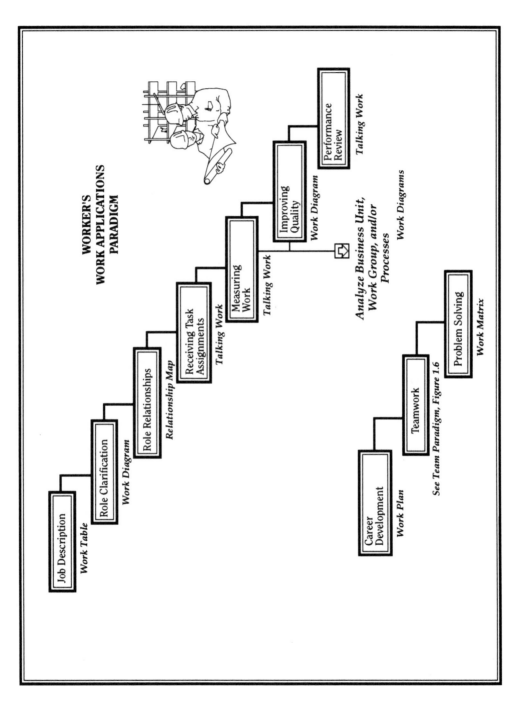

Figure 1.4

- Role relationships

- Receiving task assignments

- Measuring work

- Improving quality

- Performance review

- Career planning and development

We can see that many of the worker work applications are tied in one way or another to the work applications of a manager. In Figure 1.5, the worker and manager functions have been combined and reveal the work applications they have in common. These include work applications related to giving and receiving task assignments, measuring work, improving quality, and the like. These common applications further reinforce the need for *concurrent* (or shared) training, as opposed to the more prevalent training of managers only. Most important, they reinforce the need for a common work language between workers and managers.

Finally, we see in Figure 1.6 the Team's Work Applications Paradigm. These are work applications that relate to teams of workers and teams of workers and managers. These work applications generally include:

- Determining team roles

- Functioning as a team

- Measuring team success

- Problem solving

You can see that there are numerous messages in the world of work to which we can apply the Language of Work. In the actual process of using this work language, you will find other applications as well. What we have here, in a very true sense, is a situation where *one language fits all applications*. For example, a manager faced with performing tasks such as doing performance reviews, giving work assignments, evaluating work, leading teams, and problem solving will no longer have to learn and depend on many different "management methods"; the Language of Work will be useful for doing all these managerial tasks—"One Language Fits All."

Work Applications for the Business

So far we have only discussed applications as they relate to teams and individual workers and managers. In Chapter 2 you will be introduced to the Business Sphere.

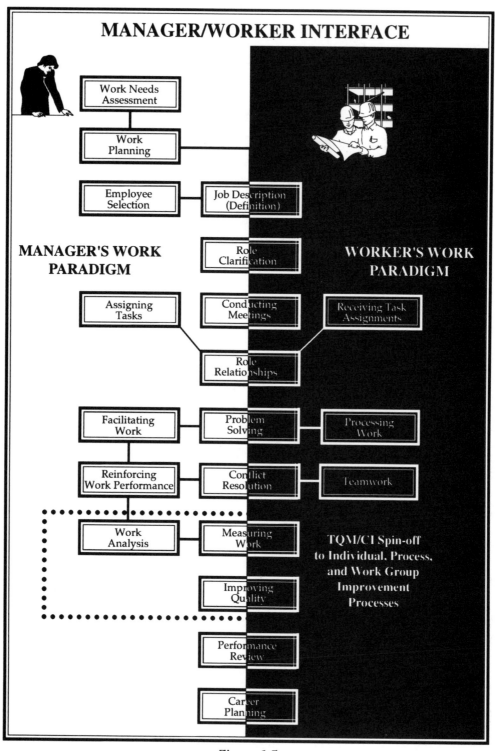

MANAGER/WORKER INTERFACE

MANAGER'S WORK PARADIGM

WORKER'S WORK PARADIGM

- Work Needs Assessment
- Work Planning
- Employee Selection
- Job Description (Definition)
- Role Clarification
- Assigning Tasks
- Conducting Meetings
- Receiving Task Assignments
- Role Relationships
- Facilitating Work
- Problem Solving
- Processing Work
- Reinforcing Work Performance
- Conflict Resolution
- Teamwork
- Work Analysis
- Measuring Work
- Improving Quality
- Performance Review
- Career Planning

TQM/CI Spin-off to Individual, Process, and Work Group Improvement Processes

Figure 1.5

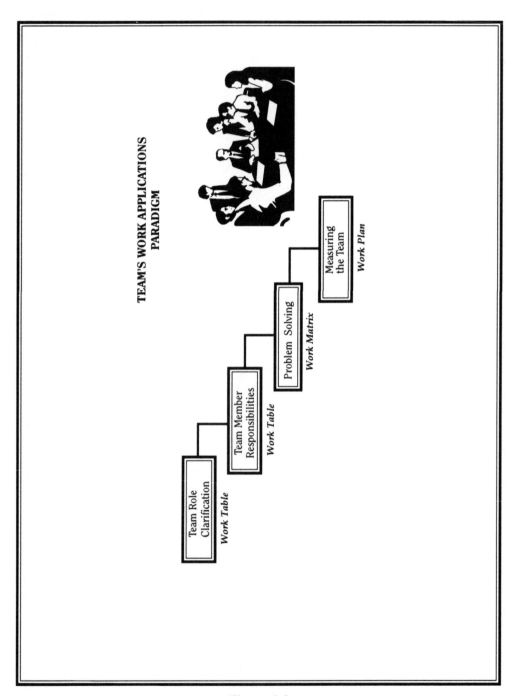

Figure 1.6

You will learn in detail how the Language of Work can also be applied to improve other major work applications as they relate to the business as a whole. These work applications include work *processes*, the work of *work groups*, and the work of the entire business as a *business unit*. In Figures 1.3 and 1.4, these other business work applications are identified by the arrow within the dotted-lined box that points to "Analyze Business Unit, Work Group, and/or Processes."

WORK APPLICATION TOOLS—THE MEDIA OF THE LANGUAGE OF WORK

Just as a language must have a medium through which people can transmit words that convey a message (e.g., writing), a work language needs functional ways through which people can communicate and use the work language. In the Language of Work the many ways to successfully use the work language are referred to as *work application tools*. There are several tools that workers, managers, and teams can use.

It is useful to think of work application tools as convenient work performance aids or job aids for managers, workers, and teams to use in doing their work and applying the Language of Work. The following is a description of the work application tools that I have found particularly useful in meeting a variety of everyday work needs.

Talking Work

One of the best applications of the new work language is "talking work"—using the language as an everyday way to talk with others about what you or they are doing on the job. For example, managers can use the work language to give work assignments, plan work, monitor work progress, and review worker performance. Workers can use it to talk to their co-workers and managers in a common language that facilitates clear understanding of needs, requirements, procedures, and performance measurement and improvements. In short, talking work will enhance the effectiveness and efficiency of all work communication. Among its many uses are these:

- Giving and following work assignments

- Conducting performance reviews

- Giving and receiving feedback while processing work

- Giving proper reinforcement for work as it is done

- Facilitating work as a manager

- Measuring the quality of work

Work Diagrams

Work diagrams* are similar to flow charts, but give us a more complete view of work. With diagrams, managers and workers can have a clear and concise visual picture of what makes up their specific job, how things flow within it, and where communication must be assured, measured, and the like. You can use them not only to diagram your own job and those of others, but to diagram the various work groups, processes used in the business, and the business unit itself. In effect, you can analyze and understand the entire business you work in, in ways you never did before.

Work diagrams are also useful for helping teams of workers and managers work together to define and understand their individual and collective roles on the team. A diagram can be used with other teams to show exactly what it is they do and how they relate to one another in their work. The most far-reaching use of diagrams is to help individuals make their own quality improvements to better meet their internal and external client needs. You can define and use the work diagram to plan your own job needs (such as career development), communicate with your manager, clarify your role with fellow workers, and so forth.

Here are several uses of work diagrams:

- To define, measure, and improve the business in its entirety as a "business unit"

- To define, measure, and improve the various work groups that comprise the "business unit"

- To define, measure, and improve the various processes used by individuals, teams, and work groups

- To define, measure, and improve the work of individuals, either on their own or in combination with other workers and the improvement systems the business has in place (e.g., TQM, continuous improvement processes)

- To identify quality improvement points

---

* The technique of diagramming was introduced to me many years ago by Dr. Ivan Horabin in *Algorithms* (Educational Technology Publications, Englewood Cliffs, NJ, 1978). Dr. Geary Rummler and Alan P. Brache's book, *Improving Performance: How to Manage the White Space on the Organization Chart* (Jossey-Bass, San Francisco, 1991) includes several useful illustrations of their version of work diagramming. Both these resources influenced my thinking as I developed the Language of Work, and they are cited here as useful resources in learning how to produce work diagrams.

Work Matrices

A work matrix provides us with a visual framework for resolving problematic work issues. It consists of two axes. The six elements of work are listed along one axis and the existing facts associated with each element are recorded on the other axis. We can then analyze each element, determine needed changes, and decide what solution(s) would work to bring about the change.

Work matrices are particularly useful for problem solving, conflict resolution, and change management. They can be used by individuals and teams to systematically view and discuss the nature of a problem and how to solve it. This greatly improves the efficiency and skill of workers and managers trying to problem-solve in a group setting (e.g., a meeting). Thus work matrices are helpful tools in areas such as:

- Problem solving

- Conflict resolution

- Change management

- Decision planning

Work Tables

A work table displays information in a clear and easily understood form, thereby facilitating communication in the workplace and the efficient use of the information by workers and managers. For example, individual jobs or the responsibilities of individuals on a team can be displayed in work tables. They are useful for clarifying the following:

- Role definitions

- Job descriptions

- Team responsibilities

Work Relationship Maps

A work relationship map shows us the role relations that do exist or should exist between the outputs within and between various work groups; then it "links" those relationships. For example, suppose one group produces an output that is used as the input by another group. If we list the outputs of each work group, we can then use line or word relationships to specify where the relationship occurs. From these relationships, measurement can be devised and carried out so that we can see if the relationships are what they should be. If they are not, then we can improve them through a variety of quality improvement interventions. Among other things, work relationship maps are helpful for:

- Role clarification between groups and individuals

- Role clarification within work groups

- Team relationship clarification

Work Plans

A work plan is a way to describe, in the Language of Work, what will be done to accomplish business plans or work goals and when, where, and how it will be done. This tool is applicable to many forms of planning. For example, a business plan for a business may be written to accord with the six elements of the work language. Measurement can also be tied to the plan so that it is possible to measure effectiveness during or following execution of the plan. Representative areas in which work plans are applicable include:

- Business planning

- Career development planning

- Job description

- Measuring team effectiveness

WHAT WILL IT TAKE TO LEARN AND USE THE LANGUAGE OF WORK?

If you have ever attempted to learn a foreign language, you know that learning a language takes practice. Although the Language of Work has relatively few terms, it still will take practice and commitment. Some people may have difficulty, for example, thoroughly understanding at first what an output is, distinguishing output from consequences, knowing what conditions really exist and influence their work, where to seek and find feedback, and what the expected consequences are. Again, learning any new language takes practice, and through use, proficiency will emerge.

As is the case with most change in business, some workers and managers will resist learning the new work language because of the initial effort it involves. And it *would* be much easier to continue the norm of insufficient communication—to be generic and unclear in our descriptions of work and the way we execute and manage work. It does take more effort to do the following:

- Specify the standards (conditions) to be followed in work

- Insist on adherence to the standards and process through feedback

- Facilitate the execution of process

- Reinforce good output and correct improper output

- Attend to the achievement of positive consequences

- Take the time to measure client satisfaction and make adjustments when and where needed

But there is no question that when work is defined more completely and we speak the same work language, many benefits to the individual worker, manager, and business do result. The effort is worth it! Here are but a few reasons why the Language of Work is so effective:

- **The work language is built on the "performance" of work rather than on work as a unit of production.**

Too often we view and measure work as if it were equivalent to a production line. Managers exhibit this mentality when, in complaining about workers, they say, "If only they would do the work, we wouldn't have the problem of getting things done around here!" This is a very short-sighted view of work. Businesses that refer to their elements as "raw material," "work," and "results" also exhibit a similar limited view of work. It too is a kind of cold production-line concept. What we have to realize is that work is performed by people, and that it therefore needs humanizing. To do this, we must shift our perspective on work to a human performance point of view. It is *the people* who produce the output, using inputs *they* obtain and manage, under conditions that *they* must adhere to, with the *help* of useful feedback that *they* seek personally or that is provided *by those other humans* who supervise the work. A common work language helps bring the humanizing element to work.

- **The work language starts with familiar terminology, and then establishes a new paradigm of understanding and use.**

Words like *output, input, process,* and *conditions* are not new to the workplace; most workers and managers already understand, at least to some extent, the basic meaning of these terms. *Feedback* and *consequences* may not be as familiar to them, but it is likely that everyone has heard these words before. This feature of the six-word lexicon makes it easier for us to introduce the language to the workplace. As many terms only require clarification, the less well known terms do not appear threatening—all of which facilitate understanding the terminology in the context of a new syntax: the Performance Paradigm.

• **The Language of Work can be used by everyone in the business.**

Unlike technical and financial language, the Language of Work is designed for use by everyone in the workplace; its benefits are not confined to one specialized group. As it has many specific applications, these benefits are far-reaching. It not only improves communication in everyday conversations about work, but affords more systematic ways to manage, plan, organize, and measure work. (Chapters 3 through 6 are dedicated to showing specific ways that the new work language can be applied.)

• **The work language provides us with a more complete view of work.**

Presently workers and managers tend to limit their view of work to outputs and process. As a result, certain critical elements are either overlooked or underemphasized when work is assigned, executed, and measured. Also, workers and managers generally are not taught the skills they need to analyze their own work and make it more effective and efficient (a situation that will be discussed in Chapter 3). Equally so, managers and workers are not taught together often enough, so that they understand and appreciate one another's problems and perspective of work. A more complete view of work results in a more complete understanding of how the individual contributes to work, which facilitates the success of programs such as total quality management. Learning and using the Language of Work together, workers and managers take the initiative to improve work and rely less on the business to make improvements.

We are now ready to learn how to apply the Language of Work.

CHAPTER 2

THE BUSINESS SPHERE

A BUSINESS PERSPECTIVE FOR USING A COMMON LANGUAGE OF WORK

Do you have a thorough knowledge of what goes on in the company you work for? Chances are you know the organization of the company reasonably well and what the company produces or services. You probably understand to some degree its production methods, and perhaps you know a bit about sales and delivery systems. But how much do you know about what others in the company do and how they do it? What about your role relationship to them? What specific company policies and procedures apply to your work? Could you identify the quality improvement needs of your job or of the company in general? Have you ever had the opportunity to explain to others in your work group exactly what your job entails and what you would like to see done better? What do you know about the overall process of the business? How difficult is it to communicate about work with others in the company? Or is such communication virtually nonexistent?

Answers to these and similar questions (like the items assessed in the Work Communications Survey you completed in the Introduction) commonly reveal that workers and managers know relatively little about the business they work for. This is not surprising since many companies devote so little time to helping the work force understand, communicate about, work on, and improve the business. Most communication is left to individual managers—managers who do not usually have a functional model of what work is, nor a language to explain work to others. Consequently, they expend most of their efforts on telling workers, "This is what needs to be done!" Or, "The work must be done!" This is not true communication about work.

The Language of Work can help us solve communication problems like these, but if we are to use the language to its fullest advantage, workers and managers must first be given a model for viewing their business from the standpoint of work. This chapter presents such a model—one that helps us understand how a business is structured to do what it does. The discussion of the model has a twofold purpose:

1. To illustrate the various levels of a business to which workers and managers can apply the Language of Work in many useful ways, either individually or in groups

2. To provide a framework that assists us in seeing how a common work language is a useful "business glue" of understanding

We will look first at the traditional way to view a business and then at a new three-dimensional view: the Business Sphere. Next, we will look at how to apply the work language at each level of the business to improve work quality. Finally, we will see how the work language provides the "business glue" that helps hold the business together and move it forward as a quality-driven culture. Those who are involved in continuous improvement processes, such as TQM, will find this view of business, the application of the Language of Work to it, and the building of an understandable work culture to be of particular interest. Perhaps for the first time, we will discover a common way for everyone to view work and improve it.

THE TRADITIONAL VIEW OF BUSINESS

Business is most often viewed as having four levels of operations in accomplishing its output(s) for customers and clients. The way to depict these levels is shown below; each level will then be described separately.

BUSINESS UNIT			
WORK GROUPS	Work Group	Work Group	Work Group
PROCESS	Process		Process
INDIVIDUALS	Individuals		Matrix

Level One: The Business Unit

Whether for profit or not, a business produces things (products, services, knowledge, and so forth) that can be called outputs. A typical **business unit** is composed of various **work groups**, within which **individuals** work together, using **processes** for the common end of producing outputs that have positive consequences for the business. Business units are not restricted in size—they can comprise a few workers and managers or up to as many as thousands of people. The word *business unit* may be used to designate the major part of a business that produces a significant output; it may also be used to designate the business as a whole. The following will make this clearer.

In the case of large corporate businesses, the whole corporation itself is the primary business unit. But there are other major business units within the larger business unit (corporation), such as various divisions, regional offices, and branch offices. Each of these produce significant outputs for the business, and usually to external clients, although the outputs may be significant ones to other business units of the corporation as well. The distinguishing feature of a business unit, therefore, is that it produces a common output of significant size that requires various work groups to work together. Here is a real-life example of a business unit.

The Morrison Knudsen Corporation, a large company that I once worked for, is itself a business unit. But it is a business unit that also has other significantly sized business units that produce outputs for clients. For example, it has construction, mining, engineering, design, railroad, operations and maintenance, and other profit units. Because these units are considered important business entities in the total context of a corporate "business," they must be dealt with in terms of how they themselves can be improved effectively and efficiently as "businesses." From a performance improvement perspective, to treat these "divisions" as anything less than a business could be a mistake. In the grand scheme of producing meaningful outputs, divisions are meaningful business units that need definition of their own. Indeed, the divisions may be more meaningful than the total business—each contributes profits to the whole, and their specific outputs have unique inputs, conditions, processes, feedback, and overall consequences. For illustrative purposes, the box that follows will represent a business unit. The box encompasses the whole entity known as a business, be it the entire business or a major division.

```
┌─────────────────────────────────┐
│         BUSINESS UNIT           │
└─────────────────────────────────┘
```

Level Two: Work Groups

Work groups are sets of individuals who are organized to work in common process-related disciplines to produce outputs. Their outputs are then used by other work groups for the good of the business unit's outputs. The outputs eventually go to external clients. A business unit typically contains several major work groups. Work groups use inputs, operate under certain business conditions, use specific processes to produce outputs, and have consequences that affect their own livelihood. They contribute to the ultimate outputs of the business unit itself. All work groups exist for a common purpose: serving the whole business unit. Organization charts typically show the major work groups of a business unit, although some will show individuals by name and title or function. None ever show the processes. In fact, organization charts never really show work as we have defined it here, as being composed of inputs, conditions, process, outputs, consequences, and feedback. Organization charts basically only show how work is to be managed for communication purposes. Organization charts are pretty useless when it comes to showing how work is done or how the business really accomplishes its outputs.

Work groups are identified on organization charts and named after their process-related discipline—for example, proposal development, marketing, sales, human resources, design, legal, engineering, civil affairs, public relations, or accounts payable. As shown in the following illustration, several work groups usually make up the typical business unit.

Business Unit		
Work Group	Work Group	Work Group

Some businesses include work groups that can be put into a special category: "ways of doing business," for example, groups whose work involves project management or construction management. What characterizes "ways of doing business" as a kind of work group is an attempt by the business to promote or form a "concept" (i.e., a team) approach to work through a formal organizational structure within the business unit. Traditional work groups, such as those cited previously, are structured by a common task, process, or function. All accountants, for example, are grouped together into the accounting work group; all lawyers into the legal department. By contrast, "ways of doing business" work groups usually have workers and managers from different disciplines. The accountant and engineer find themselves organizationally in the same work group.

Now, while well-functioning teams require more than a formal structure to make them truly act as a team, organizational structure and special recognition of function by the business unit is still important. For example, the Chrysler Corporation's platform team concept is one instance of a business unit's formal recognition and promotion of a way of doing business that is nontraditional. Recognition promotes in individuals who are a part of a special work group a unique sense of belonging, importance, and esprit de corps. Most important to the business is the functional capability it provides the group of workers so they can produce a better output on behalf of the business unit.

"Ways of doing business" are not commonly identified on an organization chart; nonetheless, they function in the same way as the more common work groups on the organization chart. In defining a business using the Language of Work, you will be able to specify, measure, and thus improve these "ways of doing business" groups.

Level Three: Processes

Processes are the approaches that work groups use to produce their outputs. They may produce the output directly to an external client, or, if they are part of a chain of work groups, they may pass off their output to other work groups as input for processing. When and where necessary, these processes must interrelate at common points. As illustrated in the following, processes occur both within and between work groups. The process in the first box, to the left, is *within* a work group. Later we will see that there are typically two kinds of processes within a work group: an overall process used by the group and individual processes used by each job. The process in the second box, to the right, is *between* two work groups.

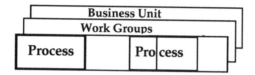

Typical processes are hiring, proposal writing, accounting, assembly, selling, prospecting, and training. Accounting is a typical process used within a work group. Proposal writing is a process that may be shared between several work groups, each of which contributes to the process. For example:

Work Group	Contribution
• Proposal Development:	Writing the proposal
• Project Management:	Project content, staffing, some writing
• Sales:	Client knowledge, presentation practice
• Training:	Presentation preparation
• Human Resources:	Resumes
• Reprographics department:	Printing, binding

All individual jobs are part of a process or processes.

Any process that is composed of systematic steps, stages, or phases can be said to be a technology. Technologies are very desirable to a business. Engineering, for example, is one such technology; it has systematic steps that the engineer follows from the beginning of a project to the very end. But many processes do not require the individual to follow systematic steps; rather, the individual carries out the process in any way he or she chooses. These nonsystematic processes are most often found in professional jobs, such as personnel and training. For example, a trainer develops a training program using the logic of what he or she thinks will work the best, rather than a technology such as Instructional Technology.

Both systematic technologies and nonsystematic processes produce outputs. However, one is better than the other in maintaining the effectiveness and efficiency of work or improving it—an important distinction. It is precisely because systematic processes use a defined procedure that is repeated over and over that the individuals using these processes tend to learn from both their successes and their mistakes; the next time they apply their technological process, they will do the job equally well or better. Also, individuals using technologies tend to associate in professional groups that research and share information to find ways to improve their technology. This, in turn, benefits the businesses who employ these individuals. By contrast, processes without systematic phases are more prone to failure and do not grow, except to a minor degree, by individual experience. For the average business, once the "experienced" individual leaves, so does a great deal, or all, of the process. The business is left to hire another "experienced" individual. By contrast, businesses built around technologies need only find another person who understands the technology, and the person's extra-added "experience" is a bonus to the business.

Fortunately for businesses and individuals, there are many nonsystematic processes that can be converted to systematic processes. For example, in the process of marketing, each person usually uses his or her personal "logic" (a nonsystematic approach) to do work. The following is an example of converting one aspect of marketing from a nonsystematic to systematic process.

In one corporation, in which I was employed as the Director of Corporate Training, the marketing development personnel had to help structure oral presentations. These oral presentations were to be given by teams that were trying to sell their services to major corporations for multimillion-dollar construction/engineering projects. Typically, these groups (as proposed project execution teams) had to give a one-hour oral presentation as the final step to potential clients selecting one of the corporations to build, design, or manage the construction/engineering of a major facility. The marketing personnel had no systematic process for developing these presentations; rather, they used whatever seemed logical to them. By contrast, the particular approach that I developed to structure, practice, and visualize presentations was very systematic, and resulted in a win ratio that was two to three times greater than any other current method being used in marketing. For marketing professionals, who were used to their own nonsystematic, "seat of the pants" approaches, the systematic approach I introduced was much more effective.

Level Four: Individuals

Individuals are, of course, the ones who do the work. In this context, they include individual workers, managers, and teams of workers and managers. As illustrated in the following, individuals use processes within and between work groups for the good of the business unit. When individuals do work between two or more work groups, they are usually working in what is called a *matrix system:* people and resources drawn from different work groups on an as-needed, project basis.

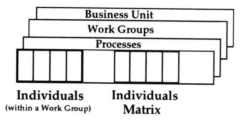

Individuals
(within a Work Group)

Individuals Matrix

Businesses often laud the importance of the individual to the success of the business. You have probably heard this before and know it to be true. But how good a mark would you give the average business in taking action to realize the full potential of its individual workers? How can a business truly account for its most important resource—the individuals?

One of the most basic things a business can do is help individuals understand *for themselves* what their function is and how it relates to others. The average worker and manager simply do not have a clear understanding of what they do. Ask any worker to state his or her job responsibilities, and you will probably receive a less than adequate answer. Ask the worker's manager to improve on the answer, and it is likely that the manager will have difficulty doing so—and difficulty providing a fully adequate statement of his or her own job responsibilities as well. If workers and managers have such problems defining their own work roles, can they really understand how their job relates to another person's job or how they could improve their own work? Are they going to know who their internal clients are? Or the satisfaction levels of the workers to whom they transfer their outputs?

Individuals need a greater understanding of their own job role, its relationship to other job roles, the process they work within, the work group they help form, and the entire business unit itself. A common work language, used on the Individual level and in relation to the other three levels of a business, will help meet that need. By using the work diagram, one of the work application tools, we can help individuals analyze their present understanding, detect weaknesses, and make improvements. I have personally used these diagrams in exercises with workers and managers, and have seen firsthand the difficulties people experience when they must diagram their own work. Invariably, when people see one another's diagrams, they are surprised to learn what others are responsible for in the workplace, and it is not unusual for individuals to learn they are responsible for something they have been unaware of. (In Chapter 3, we will take a close look at a particularly useful work-diagram exercise.)

If workers and managers are to understand how their individual jobs relate to processes, work groups, and the business unit as a whole, they must learn how to use a common work language. They must also learn how to look at a business in a new way—as an entity with several levels of work, of which they constitute one very important, but not exclusive, level. The Business Sphere, discussed next, provides a view of what a business should be. It will help us see and understand the totality of a business.

THE BUSINESS SPHERE: A THREE-DIMENSIONAL VIEW OF BUSINESS

The two-dimensional view of business described the organization and its operation as they usually prevail in most businesses today: four distinct layers of thought and action that seemingly have little in common in the mind of the work force. By contrast, the three-dimensional view to be introduced as the Business Sphere is a view of what business should be: the optimal stage of worker/manager understanding, communication, and action based on a common Language of Work.

There are three key words that characterize work in the Business Sphere:

- Position

- Perspective

- Understanding

View 1: Position

Figure 2.1 is the position view of the Business Sphere. Here one sees a series of four spheres, one inside the other, which add up to the grand Business Sphere (presented later in Figure 2.3).

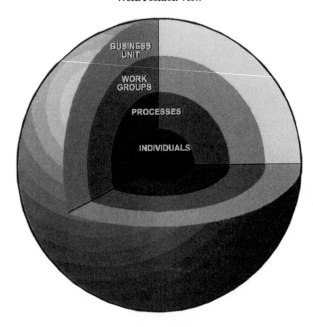

THE BUSINESS SPHERE
Work Position View

Figure 2.1

First, note that the center sphere represents individuals—workers, managers, executives, and teams. Individuals are the key to attaining business success. In terms of actually getting work done, individuals are more important than any of the other three spheres—processes, work groups, or the business unit—although all levels are needed. Without competent and content individuals, all the processes, work group organization, and business unit plans are worth only the paper they are written on. The old adage "People are our most important resource" makes a business successful only if the business follows up this claim with action. The Business Sphere, as we will discover throughout this book, places *every* individual, including the average worker, in the leading role of understanding and improving the business. For example, all individuals will be able to make quality improvements, many of them on their own and to their own job first. This is quite a contrast to the two-dimensional view, in which managers and executives typically dominate as the key resources and decision-makers as to what will be improved.

The position of processes in the Business Sphere is one of the close but proper relationship to individuals and work groups. Basic is the need to define processes as the best means to accomplish the outputs of the business unit. This may seem obvious, but in the traditional two-dimensional view, individuals are often left to determine their own process, and collectively their individual processes become the overall process for the business (this is especially true in service-oriented processes). The Business Sphere takes a new approach. Processes are defined, then individuals are selected, and finally work groups are determined and organized.

The position of work groups in the Business Sphere gives the organization the structure it needs to organize processes effectively and efficiently with the right individuals and resources. In the Business Sphere, the processes and individuals must be known first before it can be determined what work group arrangements would best help carry out the processes and utilize the talents of individuals in achieving the business unit outputs. In the two-dimensional view, the work group often dominates over processes and individuals; it is usually led by the individual manager who maintains control, even at times overriding the very processes and individuals that are there to achieve the business outputs. Such a position is counterproductive to the mission and ends of the business. When the work group position is properly understood and organized, such as in the Business Sphere, there is less likelihood of abuse, since everyone understands the best use of individuals, processes, and work groups.

The position of the business unit as the all-encompassing outer sphere is as it should be: a collection of work groups, processes, and individuals that form an entity. In the two-dimensional view, the business unit is often seen as comprising the executives who manage the business—as if the business unit were the corporate office. In viewing the Business Sphere, we will see the business unit as an integrated entity composed of major outputs as products and services, major resources as inputs, work groups that process, business conditions that influence inputs and process, major consequences that must be attended to in order to achieve client satisfaction, and major feedback loops needed to maintain constant communication. The business unit in the Business Sphere is a comprehensive body of the elements just listed, not a disparate collection of individuals, disjointed processes, or alienated work groups led by executives.

When we know position, we also know:

- The importance of our own contribution as individuals to the business

- How each level of the business contributes to and relates to the others

- What level of the business is appropriate to change in order to make improvements

The Benefits of Knowing Position

When we have a proper *position* view of business, as afforded by the Business Sphere, the following are more likely to occur:

1. Businesses will see the importance of all individuals and utilize them in the business as the core strength of the business. Without individual skills, general contentment, individual and collective contribution to quality, emphasis on being customer-driven, and the like, a business is less apt to succeed.

2. Processes will drive accomplishment, rather than individuals driving the processes.

3. Business will learn to look for needed improvements in processes and individuals before changing the organization through realignment of work groups.

4. In light of its defined goals and mission, the business unit will set the overall direction through careful definition of outputs, inputs, business conditions, processes, consequences, and feedback. The business will then define the processes, the individuals, and the work group organizational structure that are necessary to achieve its ends.

View 2: Perspective

Perspective is our view of things in our environment. In this instance, it is our view of the business we work in. Our perspective of business can be positive or negative, cloudy or clear, motivating or demotivating, energizing or draining. As is the case with our view of our personal lives, the more positive, clear, self-fulfilling the perception is, the happier we are, and the better off the business is for it. Perspective gets at the very heart of what individuals think of the business: what they like, are apathetic about, whether they move along with the status quo. Business can do a lot to improve perspective. While some of this is a function of work conditions, salary, benefits, incentives, and the like, much of perspective really has to do with what individuals know and don't know about what is going on; how much influence they believe they have; who will listen to them, value them, and care about what they do and don't do; and what is communicated.

In the two-dimensional view of business, perspective typically comes from the top. The company or its major emissaries, namely management, tell us what the business is and how things are to be done. We may even be asked to make a contribution to the business plans and to suggest improvements, and be motivated by monetary rewards, benefits, and such. But the two-dimensional view does not provide us with a way to understand the business for ourselves, a way that helps us understand our own work and the processes we use, the work group we work in, and the business unit itself. The Business Sphere provides an enhanced, clearly defined perspective.

THE BUSINESS SPHERE
Work Perspective View

Figure 2.2

Perspective in the Business Sphere is achieved through the use of a paradigm by which everyone in the organization can view *all* of the business in a common, useful, and highly utilitarian manner. In Figure 2.2 we see this represented in the Business Sphere by the arrows that transverse each of the four levels of business. Each level can be defined, executed, measured, administered, and improved upon by using the Language of Work. Thus, our perspective as individuals working for the business is increased by our using the Language of Work to view and act at each level. The view can exist no matter what level we are viewing or with whom we are interacting in the business. In the traditional two-dimensional view of business, there is no common view of work and business utilized by all the work force; when and if there is, it is usually a view held tightly by only management. The Business Sphere perspective gives everyone a clear view.

When we know perspective, we also know:

- Our job and its contribution to the business

- Our process and where we fit into other processes

- The importance of our work group and other work groups

- The business as a whole

- That we are valued and can make contributions on our own and with others

The Benefits of Knowing Perspective

1. Everyone in the business has a clear understanding of the business' overall direction and of the processes and work group organization that exist to achieve the business ends.

2. Work group relations are strengthened by work groups knowing their contributions to one another.

3. Individuals help improve quality not only in their own jobs but in all aspects of the business, because they more fully understand the business.

4. A common work language is spoken and utilized to improve individuals, processes, work groups, and the entire business unit.

5. A team approach, combined with individual initiative, is made possible by the common perspective of the Language of Work.

View 3: Understanding

Understanding is the capacity for comprehension. For instance, when we say that a person understands, we recognize that he or she can see things clearly and will act positively. In an equal sense, when we have a clear understanding of the business we are part of, we recognize where the business is headed, how it will get there, where we fit in, how to improve things, and how to satisfy our customers and ourselves. We like our business, and we thrive.

In this book we will learn that *understanding* is the combined effect afforded by knowing *position* and having *perspective*. Recall that position is knowing your position as a worker or manager. It also means knowing the use and value of processes, work groups, and the business unit as a whole. When knowing position is combined with a way to clearly *perceive* the business, we have a precise idea of what to do and how to do it. Understanding is only possible in business when an information-rich environment is created, encouraged, and reinforced. Such an environment is created by the Language of Work.

THE BUSINESS SPHERE
Work Understanding View

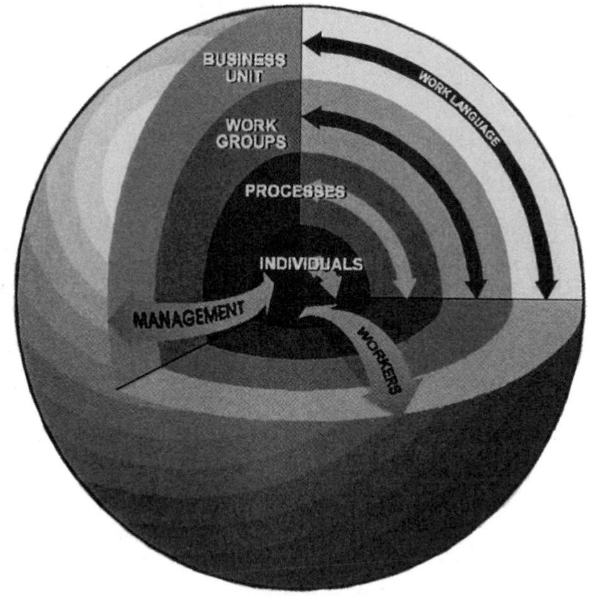

Figure 2.3

Figure 2.3 is the completed Business Sphere. Understanding is illustrated in the Business Sphere by the two arrows labeled "management" and "workers." These arrows indicate that management understands all four levels of the business. Equally so, all workers understand all four levels of the business. This understanding is largely achieved through the use of the Language of Work at all four levels to help analyze, communicate, execute, evaluate, administer, and improve work. It is also made possible by knowing the position of each level and when and where to change things for the positive benefit of ourselves and the business.

When we have understanding, we have the following:

- Equal access to the business and what is happening to it

- The ability to contribute to any area of the business that will make the business and us better

- Open and clear communication on all aspects of the business

- Better morale

The Benefits of Understanding

1. Understanding provides the "super glue" that binds the business together through comprehensive understanding and participation by everyone in the work force.

2. It reduces worker and manager stress over what the business is and what is happening to it.

3. It allows everyone to contribute to a quality-driven culture at all levels of the business.

THE FOUR LEVELS OF THE BUSINESS SPHERE AND THE LANGUAGE OF WORK

In Figure 2.3 we can see one level of the business inside the other: **Individuals** make up **processes**, **processes** are part of **work groups**, and **work groups** are part of the whole **business unit**. From the outside inward, the business unit is composed of various work groups, which use processes within and between them as performed by individuals. The following is an overview of the four levels using the Language of Work.

The Individual Level and the Work Language

One of the more illuminating exercises that managers can conduct is to ask workers what they do and how they do it. It results in a great variety of answers, most of which support the assertion that few of us really know how to describe the work we do. It's not that we don't do work! And yes, we can describe what we do in our particular occupation. But we simply cannot describe our work accurately, in terms that clearly convey how we do it, so that other individuals can fit into our own processes, help us improve, and communicate with us better. This is not really surprising since no one has taught us how to describe work. No one has ever sat down and said, "Let me show you how to describe your work as work, so that you understand it better and can help your supervisors and co-workers understand it better." If this were presently a standard practice, business life would be much better, but it is not. Now, however, we have the opportunity to initiate it.

We can begin communicating better about work by using each element of the work language to clarify for ourselves what our jobs comprise. For example, as you look at your own work, ask yourself what outputs you produce. Is your major output a product or a service or both? Be specific so that someone else would know too. What inputs do you utilize? What conditions must you understand and apply throughout the execution of your work? What is the process you use? And when finished with the process, what consequences do you feel, see, or want to occur? You see, it is possible to describe your job to someone else using the work language of inputs, conditions, process, outputs, consequences, and feedback! You will find it does help you communicate at a much higher and more meaningful level than ever before.

The Process Level and the Work Language

Unless you are a recluse in your business, you have to interact with others. In other words, all of us have clients and those who give us input. Together, we make up a process. In manufacturing, it is easy to see the process and subprocesses. In services, it is a little harder to see, but nonetheless present. For example, when I worked as a professional trainer, my process was to develop training programs. My inputs were ideas from managers and careful needs assessment analyses of business needs. My outputs were written programs, visual media, and stand-up training courses. My process was (and is) the application of Instructional Technology. Today, I am a performance technologist. While I have different inputs, conditions, process (called Performance Technology), outputs, and consequences, and I utilize a greater variety of feedback, the elements of the work language readily transfer over to this new occupation (job). Thus, each work or business process, including yours, can be described using the work language.

The Work Group Level and the Work Language

Work does not move through an organization simply because there are individuals and processes; rather, the business is organized into various work groups, either as individuals who share similar jobs or as teams that have a special way of doing projects in common. These are commonly identified as departments, sections, and so forth.

Work groups relate to one another in several ways. One way is by the output that one work group provides another work group as its input. The quality of such an output will have a direct effect on the ability of a subsequent work group to produce it own quality work. Work groups also relate through their understanding of one another. For example, when one work group wants something from another work group, its members should consider how their need pertains to other work groups that have similar or competing needs.

The Language of Work can be used to define various work groups by using the same paradigm, and therefore makes it easier to relate the similarity or differences between work groups. The work language makes it quite clear where one output becomes the input to another work group. The Language of Work goes beyond the organizational-structure view of work groups. It does this by defining how they actually accomplish their work and how they must relate that work to the work of other groups.

The Business Unit Level and the Work Language

Applying the work language to the entire business unit is quite easy. All businesses produce outputs. We generally call them *products* and *services*. Businesses also begin with inputs. We call inputs, in the general sense, *resources*, *raw materials*, *funds*, *client needs*, and even *ideas*. The conditions of the typical business unit are the rules the business has to live under, such as government rules, tax laws, ethics, public demands, and competition. The processes are how the work groups interrelate and "get the work done." Representative consequences might include new opportunities for the business unit, client satisfaction, and a feeling that we are, as Ford likes to say, "Job One!"

COMPLETING THE BUSINESS SPHERE

When managers use a common work language, the language provides them with a common "look" (i.e., a way to manage and execute work) *into* and *out* of the Business Sphere. In a similar way, when workers use that same work language, managers and workers alike are able to see how all four levels of work interrelate. In Figure 2.3, an arrow from the outside into the center of the sphere illustrates that management can look "into" the business at all four levels and, among a host of other things, understand, communicate, administer, and measure the business. In turn, workers can look from within the sphere outward and see the same picture of the business, thus gaining a better understanding of it and an operational frame of reference. As workers might like to think of it, "We know how the business works!"—perhaps for the very first time. Thus, management and workers have a common view of the business.

This common view of the business will go a long way in both improving the business and communication. I refer to this common view of business as a kind of "super business glue." A brief description of the variety of business glues, and of the Language of Work as the super business glue, will round out this introduction to the Business Sphere. Then we will look at each of the four levels of business in detail and see how you can specifically use the various work application tools to improve work applications at each level.

The Language of Work—The Super Glue of Business

Every business needs ways to bind the work force together if it is to be a vital organization. Businesses attempt this binding in any number of ways. In terms of the Business Sphere, there must be ways to bind the various levels together to meet common ends—such as profit, services, client satisfaction, and communication. These binding methods are a "business glue," and the language can be considered the "super glue of business." This super glue, more than any other business glue, does a particularly effective job in promoting business harmony. In the context of continuous improvement processes such as TQM, this super glue provides the way to build a positive "culture," because everyone is speaking a common work language.

What Are the Typical Business Glues?

Of the several kinds of "business glues" that presently exist, few bind the typical business effectively by themselves. Even fewer also provide a good perspective of how the "glue" can be used to truly improve the business on an ongoing and consistent basis. Rather, the "insides" (work groups, processes, and individuals) of a business typically seem to be at loggerheads with themselves. If you ask the typical employee if he or she thinks the right hand knows what the left hand is doing, the employee will conclude that the head is in a cloud while the body is in constant spasm.

Organization

The most common glue is the organization chart. It neatly puts resources into departments that, if only "managed" well, could get things done. Certainly organization is needed. But the most important task of a business—getting work done so that profit can be produced — is not accomplished by organization. Organization merely categorizes the business up and down on the vertical plane. When acting according to the two-dimensional view of a business, the typical organization puts a chief executive at the business unit level, selects a few vice-presidents for the work groups, assigns a few supervisors to oversee the processes, and then considers the individuals. Even attempts at organizing "teams" are still usually an organizational attempt at gluing the business together. As a professional colleague, Dr. Geary Rummler, best frames it: Businesses create silos (vertical organization) by which they attempt to run the business. Consequently, some managers only see the importance of their "silo" (work group), rather than the overall need of the business as a process of many interdependent work groups.

Organization is important principally for "talking" (mainly giving and receiving direction and facilitation) about work and for "knowing" whom to turn to. But work is not mostly talk, although communication is certainly important! Technically, work is performing—it is doing, doing, doing! It is using process to produce output in the form of product, service, or knowledge. Thus, a glue related to *doing* work, as opposed to *talking* work, would be a better glue for improving and binding the business. The organization chart of a business is a necessary glue, but not the best glue for binding the business together.

Leadership

A second kind of business glue is leadership. "If we just had effective leadership, this business would really get where it needs to be!" True, good leadership is needed. It can "model" for us as performers (workers). It can effectively "talk"—there is that talk again—and exhort us to move onward! It can plan. But it cannot do—there is that doing again—for us as performers. In a sense, leadership involves only one or a "few" persons, and good leadership is hard to find. What looks like leadership is often only an individual who thinks workers are an army and that a mere order will get them to do what is needed. Businesses are not the military. So leaders have to set the tone, but workers sing the song. These are not meant to be cute metaphors; the truth is, leadership can go only so far to bind a business together. So, while leadership is important, to some degree it is not the best answer for improving and holding the business together.

Vision

How about the current popular glue known as vision? Like organization and leadership, vision has an important role in business. Good visions, backed by action, can hold a business together and give it common direction. I am certain that the young people who believed in Microsoft stuck together in their vision to make it work. Typically, though, people can stick with only so much vision; then it is business as usual. And as with leadership, vision can only lead; it can not perform! Vision goes only so far in improving and binding the business.

Skilled Work Force

A fourth popular glue is the skilled work force. Businesses that use this glue, like Xerox and IBM, rely on such methods as extensive training, team building, and sending their managers to "ranches" to climb mountains, ford rivers, and participate in other outbound activities to test and bring forth their character and self-worth. These techniques build the work force into a united front that helps carry the business forward. To a degree, the skilled work force can become a strong glue. Yet, while this glue may involve many more in the business than previously described glues, it too is limited in holding the business together. Fundamentally, developing a skilled work force is an attempt at developing the individual and team, but it has little to do with their understanding the business itself and how the business can be improved; rather, it is letting individuals understand themselves and others.

Policies and Procedures

One of the more interesting business glues is the combination of policies and procedures. Business after business has attempted to capture in writing the rules, regulations, guidelines, and procedures that they think should "govern" the way things will be done in the business. Often you can hear a manager say of workers: "If only they would follow policy and procedure, this company would not have the problems it has." To a degree this is true. But one only need point to the policies and procedures that are ignored by the work force and management, or to the number of businesses that closely guard the distribution of these documents, lest they fall into the hands of everyone in the work force—a concern that escapes logic.

Policies and procedures are a convenient and needed reference source, but they certainly do not get work done or consistently get workers to do work better. The reasons the work force ignores or does not read the policies and procedures are numerous. More important is the realization that there is probably no way in the world to get the work force to keep these "rules" before them. Yes, the work force can be encouraged, but no, they will not consistently follow the rules. So, as a manager, you can pretty well stop sending out memos admonishing people to follow the rules! Your best bet is to tie the policy or procedure directly to when it is to be used and then reinforce its actual use—both uses of which will be elaborated upon later in this book. Polices and procedures are really not a very effective business glue.

Other Glues

There are other "glues" whose results are similar to the five glues already described. While useful and necessary for their individual contribution, they do not get work done, nor do they describe work in a form useful for overall business improvement. These include such glues as common goals, culture, unique product or service, strategies, reputation, unions, location, good benefits, promises of longevity, and technologies.

The Need for a Better Business Glue

Where does this bring us? Is there a better option? A better business glue? And what would it do for business that the other glues couldn't? Certainly, we need a better business glue! In particular, we need a business glue suited to improving the business immediately and on a continuous basis. One that explains and illustrates work would be particularly useful. One through which the business can be continuously improved would be dynamite. We need a kind of super glue that everyone can understand and use to make the business better. This super glue would give all the work force (workers and management) a common insight into the purpose of the business and provide a broad application of how to administer, operate, improve, and measure the business.

What we need is a succinct, systematic way to define a business unit, work groups, processes, and the work of individuals—the four business levels. Otherwise, business will be carried on in a more random fashion (as is currently the case) and be closed to ways to measure it for ongoing improvement And if those at all the four levels of business could use the same model, they would be more apt to understand how work is accomplished and could interrelate the work and make improvements. For example, the more traditional ways of making assessments and improvements, such as the individual thoughts and actions of managers, will no longer do. Project and business plans that are defined in strictly content terms, generic goals, and targets will no longer suffice. These plans may be defined clearly (with definable dollar targets), but they are useless if the rest of the business does not have a model to achieve the market goals. The simple truth of the matter is that individuals plan well for others, but the others don't always follow.

The Language of Work is the super glue that makes it possible to communicate more effectively and improve the business. When individuals (workers and managers) at all levels understand and use this glue, the business is more tightly bound by such positive elements as a common understanding of the purpose of the business, the knowledge of where the business is headed, a working understanding of processes and work groups that will be used, and a clear idea of where each person fits within the business. We are now ready to see specifically how to apply our new work language.

CHAPTER 3

APPLYING THE LANGUAGE OF WORK TO INDIVIDUALS

We begin by examining the various applications of the work language to business at the level of Individuals, such as yourself and those with whom you work. Once you understand the application as a worker or manager, it is far easier to see the application to processes, work groups, and the entire business unit.

Before we start, though, it is important to note that when we use the work language to redefine a current business, it is usually preferable to start at the Business Unit level, then move on to processes, individuals, and finally the work groups. Why? Because we must DEFINE AUSTRALIA FIRST, that is, define our target first. This means defining the purpose of the business before doing anything else. Only then can we define the supporting processes needed, specify which individuals will carry out the processes, and determine how these individuals will be organized into effective and efficient work groups. I am introducing you to the applications of the Language of Work by starting at the Individual level only because it is easier to understand and see the power of the work language when applied to yourself rather than to the business unit, its processes, or work groups.

If there is one level of business where large potential gains are possible, it is the Individual level, which includes managers, workers, and teams of individuals. The old adage "People are our most important resource" is true, even if we have not found particularly highly effective and efficient ways to utilize that resource and make people truly feel "most important." Lately, efforts such as integrated work teams and total quality management for continuous improvement have helped, but they have not proven to be the complete answer. Perhaps this is because business has (1) failed to show the individual where he or she fits into the Business Sphere, and (2) failed to provide the means and motivation for individuals to undertake their own improvement *on their own*. Individual initiative is, after all, a very powerful force for business improvement if leaders allow and encourage it. Many business leaders, unfortunately, do not know how to do this, and workers become too discouraged to take initiative. Using the Language of Work can help restore initiative because it shows the individuals how to diagram, measure, and make their own improvements.

Several years ago a German colleague taught me a lesson that has since served me both in my personal growth and professional life. I was at the University of Gottingen, West Germany. My research was to devise an instructional design selection system that could be used by trainers to match the best teaching and learning methods to the particular needs of students and trainees in business and education. I had just finished editing a 40-volume series on various education and training methods (called instructional designs), so I was pretty well steeped in the capabilities of teaching and learning methods. Nonetheless, I struggled and struggled at this task, until one day my colleague asked a very simple question: "How did you learn to select teaching and learning methods yourself?" While my colleague did not know how to do the task himself, he certainly knew what questions to ask! By answering that question I was able to go on and develop the selection system. Instead of needing to look outside myself (for processes and understanding), I needed only to look inside myself at my own experience. The lesson I learned can be applied to the improvement of the individual worker, manager, or team. The answer is a matter of taking charge of one's own job—not always relying on a boss or business for directions. Depending on others in business to "figure it out," to tell you to take "the responsibility," is all too frequent in business. If you can figure it out yourself, not only do you get better at your own work and work better with others, but you become more innovative and creative in the process. You are freed, in a true sense, to make your own contribution and feel good about it. You are also in a position to communicate more clearly with your manager about your developmental needs and work needs. Any manager would appreciate a worker who can communicate well about work. Let us look closely at one work application tool—the work diagram—to see how this is done.

LEARNING TO USE THE WORK LANGUAGE ON THE INDIVIDUAL LEVEL: WORK DIAGRAMS

If workers and managers are to learn how to apply the work language on the Individual level, it makes sense for them to begin by focusing on their most immediate concern in the workplace: their own work—what they as individuals do and how they do it. The work diagram is a particularly useful work application tool for helping workers and managers look closely at their work and, as mentioned in Chapter 2, analyze their present understanding of their jobs. In this way, they can detect weaknesses in their understanding and make improvements.

There are many advantages to "initiating" the application of the work language on the Individual level by using work diagrams. When we use the Language of Work in our diagramming, we not only produce a meaningful description of the job that we, as individuals, do, but fully illustrate the fundamental dimensions of the work language. We identify in *specific words* the six work elements—our inputs, conditions, process, outputs, consequences, and feedback—and present them in an orderly manner, according to the *syntax* of the Performance Paradigm. Our *message* is a clear definition of the job, which we can understand and communicate to anyone else in the business—especially when they know the Language of Work as well.

Another advantage is that the work diagram itself is a product—something substantial and meaningful that, in facilitating clear communication, underscores the power of the work language and helps erode any initial resistance to the work language. Workers will discover that they can diagram their work for their own use, then for use with others, such as co-workers, workers in other work groups that share input and output relationships, and managers who facilitate work, provide and seek feedback, and encourage positive consequences. Of course, managers also benefit from diagramming their work and sharing it with others. The following exercise will help you understand how invaluable this application tool is for introducing the work language and defining the work language for individuals.

Defining the Work Language on the Individual Level: An Exercise

To introduce you to the use of the work language for the individual, I would like you to diagram your present job as I show you a diagram for one of the sample job positions used throughout this book—that of Lee, the proposal writer. Write your name and job title in the box that follows, just the way the proposal writer's name appears in the sample illustration.

Your Work Diagram

> LEE
> Proposal Writer

LEE'S Work Diagram

Now, to the right of the box, list all the outputs that you produce from your present job. Outputs, you will recall, include various services, products, facts, and knowledge. You may wish to refer to Figure 1.1 again (page 4) for the definition and typical sources of the six words that compose the Language of Work. List the specific tangible outputs you produce. Here is one helpful approach: Imagine that you had to carry or deliver your outputs to someone else. Label what they would look like. For example, the outputs for Lee's job would include the written proposal document, cost proposal documentation, written qualification descriptions, and oral presentation assistance in the form of visuals, outlines, and handouts. These outputs would be written to the right of the job title as follows:

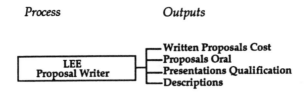

LEE'S Work Diagram

Another useful approach for determining outputs focuses on the customer. Think of who your customers are. Once you have identified them, then ask, "What it is that they need, want, or expect from me in the form of a product, a service, or knowledge?" For internal clients, these outputs are typically things they need to do their own jobs. For example, John will need the output of Lee's proposal writing (e.g., the cost figures on project items) to do his job as an engineer.

Now, returning to your personal diagram, list to the left of your job title any of the inputs you are provided or must obtain to do your job. Inputs typically include client needs, people, ideas, equipment, facilities, funds, and information. For Lee's work diagram, the following inputs are listed:

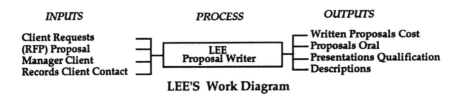

LEE'S Work Diagram

Next, list the conditions that would have an impact on your use of the inputs and the process you employ to turn your inputs into outputs. You can write these in a space above the inputs and process. Remember, conditions are the factors that influence the use of inputs and processes, and that you cannot change. For example, rules, company policies, and government regulations are examples of conditions. For Lee, conditions typically include business policies, government regulations, perhaps a proposal-writing style manual, and competition. Competition might at first seem like an unusual condition, but competition, in the example of the proposal writer, would influence inputs like pricing, methods used, and other aspects of inputs and processes. The conditions for Lee's proposal writing position are listed below:

CONDITIONS

Government Regulations
Business Policies
Proposal Guideline
Manual Competition

Next, make a list of the consequences that result from your producing the outputs under the prevailing conditions. Consequences are the effects an output has on a person, product, service, or situation. You can easily identify consequences by asking the following two questions: (1) What does your output do for your business? (2) How do you feel about what you produce? The answers are consequences. For now, list your consequences in the following space. Later we will see how to incorporate this list into the work diagram.

Consequences

-

-

-

-

-

For comparison, here is a list of expected consequences for Lee, against which you can compare your list. Make sure your list includes only consequences and no outputs. Remember, consequences result from the outputs you have produced.

Sample Consequences for Lee

- Contributing new work to the business

- Personal satisfaction in "winning the job"

- Building a team while working with others in the proposal writing effort

- Client satisfaction (particularly if the job is won)

- The satisfaction of others, such as his supervisor

As you can see, proposal writers typically achieve consequences related to client satisfaction, the sense of "winning" new work, and the pleasure of working with others in a team relationship. Whenever you hear individuals complain about their work, you can bet that they are complaining about the lack of positive consequences. By attending to inputs, process, conditions, and feedback, you can change negative consequences to positive consequences. This "attending" to different elements of the work language to produce positive consequences is but one of the many benefits of knowing and using a common work language.

We have just about finished the work diagram. The only remaining element is feedback. In one sense, feedback completes the work cycle; it is a response to outputs that lets us know whether things have been done right or need to be adjusted (for example, the reaction from your client when you deliver your output). Remember, there are two kinds of feedback. One is provided once the output is finished; the second is provided during the course of processing the output. An example of the second kind would be information your manager gives you during processing to improve the process for a better output. In the space below, list the forms of feedback you currently receive and would like to receive; then compare your list to the list of feedback for Lee's job.

Feedback

HAVE   LIKE TO HAVE

Feedback After Output

- •   •
- •   •
- •   •
- •   •

Feedback During Processing

- •   •
- •   •
- •   •
- •   •

LEE'S Feedback

Feedback After Output
- • The proposal a good (bad) proposal
- • External client acceptance of the proposal
- • A third party edits the proposal

Feedback During Processing
- • Someone to proofread the final proposal copy
- • Feedback from Proposal Manager while writing the proposal

Now that you have completed this exercise, you should have a rough diagram of your job and a better idea of how to define work more completely by using the Language of Work. To facilitate work diagramming by workers and managers, however, requires further knowledge of how we construct a diagram and individualize it with the specific outputs, inputs, conditions, process, consequences, and feedback of our work. It is also helpful to see how a diagram can be presented in graphic form for a clear understanding of the job as a whole. The following section provides these additional details on the use and construction of work diagrams on the Individual level.

DIAGRAMMING WORK ON THE INDIVIDUAL LEVEL

When we construct a work diagram, it is essential to use a particular approach and to deal with each of the six work elements in a certain order. Because we must always define our target first, the order in which we approach and define the specific work elements of a job must accord with this basic principle; however, the syntax of the Performance Paradigm still rules the actual structure of the diagram. This important point will become clearer as we further examine work diagramming, but is worthy of special emphasis here.

The work diagram of Lee, the proposal writer, is presented in graphic form in Figure 3.1, and will be used to illustrate the discussion. Similarly drawn work diagrams for John, the CAD engineer, and Monica, the trainer, conclude this section in Figure 3.2 and Figure 3.3, respectively. They provide us with further illustrations of how, through work diagramming and the Language of Work, we can comprehend our work clearly and communicate our understanding to others.

Output

We always begin the specification or clarification of a job by determining the outputs first. We need to know what the targets are—another instance of the need to DEFINE AUSTRALIA FIRST.

Outputs, as previously noted, are the services, products, or knowledge that one produces in the job. There are different ways in which you can determine your outputs, but generally this is best done with a group of fellow workers and your manager from within the same work group. It is also recommended that you include your customers (if possible) and suppliers in the definition of your job. They lend a perspective to your work that might otherwise be overlooked by you or your immediate work group.

In addition to using others in and outside your work group to define your outputs, you might wish to use the existing job descriptions in your company. The

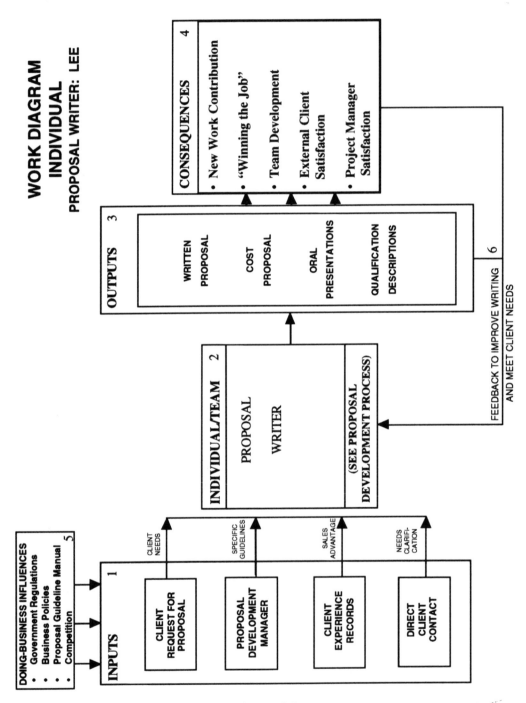

Figure 3.1

major accountabilities or responsibilities that are usually written in job descriptions generally represent outputs. For example, one of the proposal writer's outputs is found in the following job description:

> "Writes cost proposals that meet (a) client needs relative to the written proposal, and (b) the business needs relative to generating profit."

From this job accountability in the job description, we can see that one of the outputs is "cost proposals." It is a product. Other accountabilities in the job description will suggest other outputs. One note of caution, however: While job descriptions are useful resources for identifying outputs, they may be misleading at times. For example, a job description may say that an accountability of a manager is to "produce profit." But profit is not an output; rather, it is a consequence. Job descriptions that specify this kind of accountability are correct as job descriptions, on the one hand, but misleading for our purposes. Later, you will learn how to write an accurate job description based on the Language of Work approach. Just be cautious in what you read and how you use a job description. The job description may help you think of outputs (and other work elements) that you have simply forgotten about or taken for granted.

Sources for determining outputs include other workers with the same job, clients, contracts that specify deliverables, managers, fellow workers, job descriptions, and, of course, your own knowledge.

In Figure 3.1, the work diagram for Lee's job as a proposal writer, we can see that the outputs, reproduced below, are placed on the right side of the work diagram.

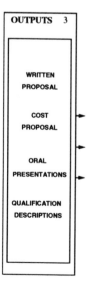

Inputs

In the broader sense, inputs for individuals represent the "raw material" that individuals receive (or access), and which they process to produce outputs. Referring back to the definition of work elements in Figure 1.1, we see that inputs generally include people, ideas, equipment, facilities, funds, information, specific requests, and the like. Other common inputs would be client needs, technologies, business plans, and project needs. These are generally easy to determine. The only caution is to make sure that you do not mix conditions with inputs. The distinction is simple: Conditions are those things that the individual cannot change or, at a minimum, can only influence in a general way; inputs, on the other hand, can be used, changed, manipulated, and in some instances ignored (though this is not a good idea).

Inputs, such as these for a proposal writer, are located in a work diagram on the left side, as can be seen in Figure 3.1.

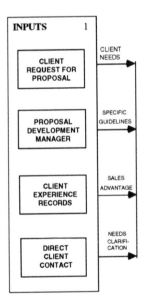

Conditions

For individuals, teams, work groups, processes, and even the whole business, conditions represent the guidelines, including restrictions, according to which the inputs are used to produce outputs through a process. In Figure 3.1, conditions are listed in a box in the upper left corner. They are identified as:

DOING-BUSINESS INFLUENCES
• Government Regulations
• Business Policies
• Proposal Guideline Manual
• Competition   5

As you can see in this example, without conditions the proposal writer would be unrestricted in what he writes. But this is not the case in business. Indeed, there are written conditions (e.g., policies and procedures) and unwritten conditions that govern all of business, even if the condition is an economic constraint. As was shown in Figure 1.1, conditions may include rules, policies, environmental conditions, and attitudes.

As a point of practical consideration, you can restrict your specification of conditions to those with which the individual must be directly concerned in the execution of the job. Specify what is practical and needed, rather than identifying every possible "general" condition. For example, specifying the important things to know about the competition is far more useful than simply stating a condition as "competition."

Consequences

Given the outputs that you are to produce, what results are expected by the business *and* for you personally? Typically these results, or consequences, range from the very specific to the more general. Here are the consequences for the proposal writer, as shown in Figure 3.1:

CONSEQUENCES   4

• New Work Contribution

• "Winning" the Job

• Team Development

• External Client
  Satisfaction

• Project Manager
  Satisfaction

In the example, a specific consequence for the proposal writer is the satisfaction of knowing that a new contract has been awarded the business based on his personal work. A general consequence is that the company is stronger. The former is far easier to measure and "feel" than the latter; however, both are important.

59

Consequences are best defined after outputs, inputs, and conditions, but before process and feedback. The reason for this is that you need to know the direction (outputs) of the work, what resources (inputs) are available, and what controls (conditions) will have an impact on the outputs and inputs before you can decide what consequences are possible and wanted. Feedback will generally be used to help encourage or reinforce consequences. Consequences are therefore specified immediately following outputs, inputs, and conditions; and feedback is specified after consequences.

Process

Perhaps you have noticed that in Lee's diagram, Figure 3.1, details are not specified for the process. This is because processes are defined before individual jobs—if the sequence of business unit, processes, individuals, and work groups is followed as suggested in Chapter 4. Normally, when the individual reaches this step and knows the process, it is recommended that the individual review the process with his or her manager in order to confirm mutual understanding of the process. Doing so will also make the final step of detailing the mutual use of feedback more definitive and meaningful.

Feedback

For individuals and teams, feedback is perhaps the single most neglected of the six elements of the Language of Work. Feedback lets the individual or team know whether they are doing (or have completed) the right things or need to make corrections.

Feedback can be freely given, not so freely given, or sought after. When freely given and freely received, it is usually perceived as constructive for the use of the process and helps produce a better output and set of positive consequences. When not so freely given, confusion can abound as to whether the process is being used correctly, whether the output is right, and whether consequences are being reinforced. When feedback is sought, it often indicates that the individual or team is hungry to be reinforced, even when process, output, and consequences are perhaps perfect. Thus, feedback is something that must be planned for and attended to on a continuous basis if it is to occur and produce positive results for individuals and teams. As was listed in Figure 1.1, typical feedback includes client reactions, information needs, and reinforcements.

In a work diagram, feedback appears in two ways. In Figures 3.1, 3.2, and 3.3, the first kind of feedback is indicated by an arrow that appears from the output and moves back into the process. It looks like this:

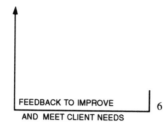

FEEDBACK TO IMPROVE
AND MEET CLIENT NEEDS   6

There is a second kind of feedback that is normally found in a work diagram, but not so readily apparent in work diagrams for individuals. This is the type of feedback found within the steps of a process. For example, suppose a proposal development manager reviews a draft version of a proposal and gives comments to the proposal writer. This would be feedback while processing. This type of feedback will be discussed in greater detail in subsequent chapters.

For further examples of work diagrams for individuals, please see Figure 3.2 and Figure 3.3, presented on the following pages.

Sharing Your Work Diagram With Others: An Exercise

There are a number of advantages to having individuals personally construct their work diagrams in a group setting that encourages sharing, rather than having a third party (such as a human resources department or a manager) construct their diagrams for them. Role clarification and confirmation of job requirements are just two of the useful outcomes. When diagramming is conducted with others in the same work group and related work groups, such as the clients and suppliers, added benefits are realized.

The method recommended for doing this is simple:

1. Bring individuals together by work group (and related work groups). Introduce them to defining work through the use of work diagrams, supplying examples.

2. Distribute felt-tipped markers and sheets of flip-chart paper. Ask them to write down their name and job function (title, area, and so forth) in the middle of a flip-chart sheet and to draw a box around them.

3. Ask them to list their various outputs—what they consider their personal accountabilities to be—to the right of the box.

4. Guide the group through the work diagramming, defining (a) inputs, (b) conditions, (c) consequences, and (d) feedback.

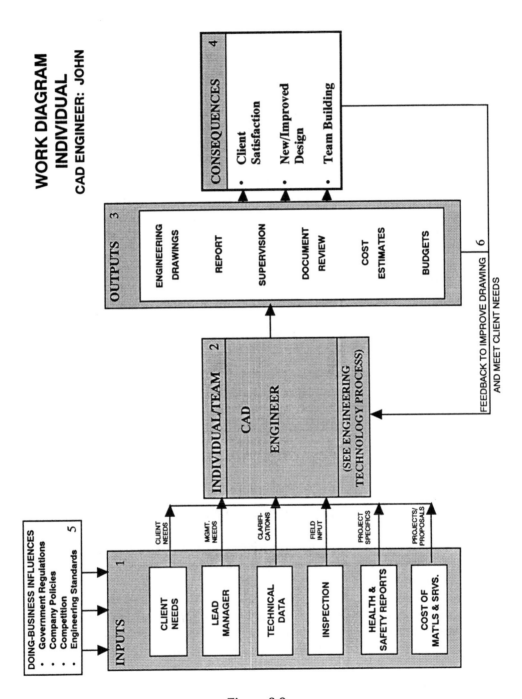

Figure 3.2

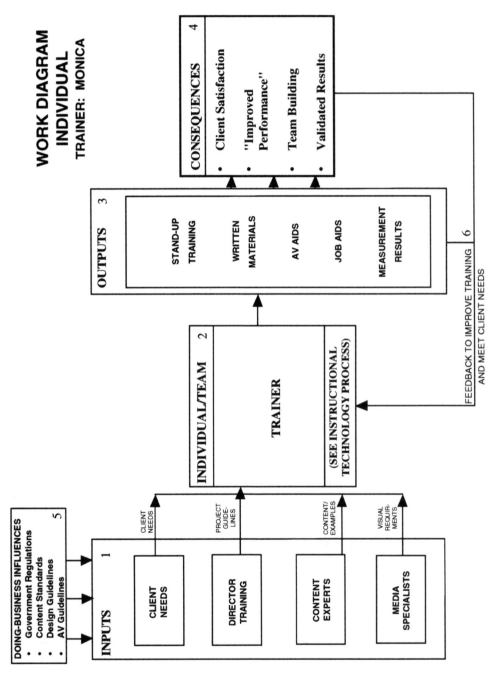

Figure 3.3

5. The individuals then share their diagrams with others in their work group and with managers. Each individual stands to present his or her diagram and is given feedback by the group and facilitator. Corrections and additions to the diagram are made as needed.

6. If time allows, it is worthwhile to look at the relationships among the various workers; for example, whose output becomes another worker's input, or who needs feedback from whom.

USING WORK APPLICATION TOOLS TO IMPROVE WORK ON THE INDIVIDUAL LEVEL

Figure 3.4 provides an introduction to the many work applications of the Language of Work that can be used by individual workers (the ones who do the primary work), managers (the ones who facilitate workers doing the work), and teams. Uses for workers and managers are categorized under the six elements of the work language. As usual, we will begin with a look at output.

USING THE LANGUAGE OF WORK
Manager and Worker Roles

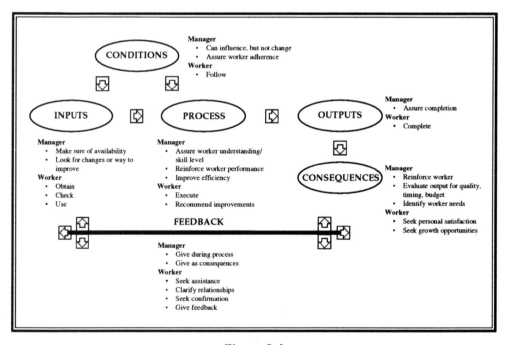

Figure 3.4

Outputs

The worker's main function is to produce output to a final stage of completion. This is, after all, what workers are employed to do—produce output. In contrast, the manager's main function is to *assure* completion. This does not include "producing" the output as a manager, although many managers feel they must do so. This distinction is important in ensuring the smoothest working of the entire organization. Managers often try to do the work for the workers, but a manager's job is to facilitate workers in doing their work—that is, set direction, remove barriers, provide feedback and guidance, and give rewards for work well done. By closely examining the outputs of individuals and the other five elements of a work diagram, the manager or supervisor can do a superb job of facilitating the work, rather than interfering with it. The manager "facilitates" the output, and the worker "completes" the output. Knowing the Language of Work helps managers understand much more clearly their job as a facilitator.

Inputs

The manager makes sure inputs are available and looks for changes in their availability or quality that might affect the worker's use of the inputs. A good manager also seeks ways to improve the delivery (timeliness) or quality of the inputs. Workers obtain, check, and use the inputs.

Conditions

The manager assures that conditions such as policies and procedures are respected by workers, and changes conditions if they adversely affect input and process. However, there is often a real problem in assuring that conditions are met, which prompts the frequently heard comment from managers: "If we could only get the workers to follow company policies and procedures, we would not have the problems we have!" Yet, remember that old saying "Out of sight, out of mind"? Well, it especially applies to business policies and procedures. I have worked in at least three major corporations where employees typically had no reason to read and follow the standard policies and procedures, no matter how well they were written or how strongly managers insisted on them. These often-huge volumes of policy and procedure manuals are needed but are not functional on a daily basis; they are much too removed from the actual work (performance) of the everyday tasks. But the introduction and use of a work language can help, and here is how.

Whenever as a manager you set about to give and discuss work assignments, follow the six elements of the work language—talk the language! That is:

- Describe the *output(s)* you expect to have produced.

- Describe the *inputs* that will be used.

- Specify the *conditions* that must be followed.

- Outline the *process* to follow.

- Agree on the *consequences* to anticipate.

- Agree on when and where *feedback* will be given or required.

Use of the work-language syntax reminds you to review with the worker what policies and procedures (and other conditions) will need the worker's attention. Thus, there is an increased likelihood that the worker will follow the conditions. When the worker complies, if you reinforce the behavior (a form of feedback), the worker will be more likely to follow the condition again in the future. (The above method of talking work will be explained in greater detail in subsequent sections of this chapter.)

Process

The worker's first responsibility is to execute the process, and second, recommend improvements in the use of the process. The manager assures that the worker understands the process and has the skills to perform the process. The manager also helps improve efficiency and provides reinforcement of success or correction during execution.

Consequences

The manager evaluates the output for quality, timing, and budget. The manager also identifies worker needs during the consequences as they relate to any interaction of inputs, conditions, and process. Finally, the manager finds opportunities in the consequences that can be used for the next step of providing reinforcement as a form of feedback. The work is structured so that the worker realizes positive consequences such as personal satisfaction in a job well done, reinforcement for doing the job better, and growth opportunities for development in his or her career.

Feedback

The manager uses feedback during process execution and in relation to consequences. Workers use feedback to seek assistance during processing, to clarify their relationship with others whom they will be working with or giving output to, and finally, to seek confirmation that they are doing things the right way during process.

Now that we have completed this overview of the use of the common work language and worker and manager roles, we can proceed to describe specific applications for workers and managers. Following this, a description for teams of individuals will also be included.

Uses of the Work Language for Workers

- **Role Clarification**   *Tool: Work Diagram or Work Table*

The notion that individuals should take charge of their own destiny rather than rely on anyone else (including the business) is well founded. Each of us should take the personal initiative to make many things happen for us and for the business as a whole. One highly useful effort is to apply a work diagram to your own job. In doing so, clarification can be achieved in the following:

1. What *inputs* you are provided or need

2. What *conditions* you are expected to function under, and what standards you must meet

3. Where you fit into a *process*, and what you use as a *process*

4. What specific *outputs* you are responsible for

5. What *consequences* can be expected

6. Where and what kind of *feedback* is required and should be sought out

Often workers lack a clear picture of their job role simply because they do not fully understand some aspect of their job accountabilities. In a sense, there is an incomplete operational description of the position. When they develop a definition for their job using a work diagram or work table (see Figure 3.5), workers and managers more fully understand for themselves their account-abilities (outputs) as defined in light of inputs, conditions, process, conse-quences, and feedback. A review of any one of the work diagrams in Figures 3.1 through 3.3 readily shows you how the definition of work using a com-mon work language communicates role clarification very well. Role clarifi-cation in these three work diagrams also goes so far as to show the relation-ship (syntax) of the various parts of a job, and when other jobs, processes, work groups, and the business unit itself are diagrammed, one can have com-plete and accurate role clarification of every aspect of the business.

WORK-TABLE JOB ROLE DEFINITIONS

	JOHN	LEE	MONICA
ELEMENT	**CAD ENGINEER**	**PROPOSAL WRITER**	**TRAINER**
Inputs	Client needs Lead manager Technical data Inspections H & S reports Cost of mat'ls & srvs.	Client needs Proposal manager Client Experience files Direct client contact	Client needs Director-training Content experts Media specialists
Conditions	Company policies Government regs. Competition Engineering standards	Company policies Government regulations Proposal guidelines Competition	Company policies Content standards Design guidelines AV guidelines
Process	Engineering Budgeting	Writing Costing	Oral presentation Writing Instructional Technology
Outputs	Engineering drawings Reports Supervision Document review Cost estimates Budgets	Written proposal Cost proposal Oral presentation Qualification descriptions	Stand-up training Written materials AV aids Job aids Measurement results
Consequences	Client satisfaction "New/Improved Design" Team building	Client satisfaction "Winning the Job" Team development New work contribution	Client satisfaction "Improved Performance" Team building Validated results
Feedback	Client reaction Manager	Client reaction Manager Client debriefing	Trainee/Mgr. reaction Director Measurements

Figure 3.5

• Role Relationships   *Tool: Work Diagram*

Rare is the worker who operates in a vacuum. Extensive is the confusion between workers within and between work groups. When each worker does his or her own work diagram, checks it out with management, and then shares it with others, a great degree of clarity can develop between workers in the business. The work diagram exercise is an excellent way to facilitate this clarity. Workers often receive positive feedback for their efforts and clarification of their own role and how it relates to others in the workplace. Questions are typically asked to help the group understand specific aspects of a person's definition of his or her work. Other questions are asked, such as how one position relates to another and why what is missing in one diagram appears in another. In essence, workers use a common work language to communicate with one another. Particularly valuable in these group discussions is the role relationship clarification that usually occurs between managers and workers.

• **Measuring Your Effectiveness**   *Tool: Talking Work*
   and Efficiency

Workers and managers are generally reluctant to ask others for an evaluation of their performance. Much of this is due, of course, to the privacy with which we surround our work and personal worth. We do not really know what to ask someone else in order to measure our work. We fear hearing a negative report, or feel we can do nothing to change the behavior that prompted the criticism. With a common work language between us, we have a framework for seeking information to measure our personal effectiveness and efficiency. But why would we want to do this?

The answer is twofold: (1) to take it upon ourselves to make our own improvements in what we do, and (2) to make improvements and adjustments before someone else tells us we have to and uses that information for such things as salary and position changes—up, down, or out. But, what do we measure?

The first thing we should look at are our outputs (DEFINE AUSTRALIA FIRST). We should ask our internal clients and external clients (if we deal directly with them) how satisfied they are with our outputs. What do they see as the quality and timeliness of our outputs? We also want to measure and assess the other work elements:

1. How well the *inputs* are being provided

2. How clear the *conditions* are, and how well we are attending to them

3. How good the *process* is

4. How well *consequences* are being achieved

5. How well *feedback* is being received and solicited

These are elements we can assess as individuals if we take the time and effort and know what to look for, and we can know what to look for if we understand and apply the work language. Once problems are found, we take it upon ourselves to make improvements. For example, if we find that an input is late, we open the communication lines with those who provide the input to see what can be done to make it more punctual. If the process is not right, we can suggest how to make it better. If the conditions are not clear, we can seek clarification. If feedback is inadequate to motivate us or help in the processing of tasks, we can communicate these to our management and seek more and better feedback. And if consequences are not what the client expects and do not meet our personal satisfaction, we can work with management (and do certain things ourselves) to look at various work elements for improvement. When we have a work language in common with others (colleagues and management), we have the means to make effective communication possible. To merely sit back, complain to another worker, or excuse problems as management responsibility will do nothing except support "business as usual."

• **Career Development**	*Tool:* ***Work Diagram***
	Work Table
	Work Plan

Career development is one arena in which self-development is in order and in which the work language can be highly useful. While career development broadly means going from one position to another, the more immediate aspect of developing your career should occur in learning and practicing specific accountabilities (outputs) of another position. And part of that learning and practicing is knowing what inputs, conditions, process, consequences, and feedback are involved in another position. If you know your own work diagram or work table and that of a co-worker, you can more clearly "see" and "understand" what someone else does in his or her work. Therefore, you can more easily plan learning an element (e.g., an output) of someone else's job.

You can (with the planning and encouragement of your manager if needed) select an output of another position and work towards its achievement with the cooperation of the worker who is currently performing that output. For instance, John, the CAD engineer, wants to learn some of the skills in proposal writing. He knows this would be useful if and when he becomes a project manager. So, he contacts Lee, one of the proposal writers, and they review Lee's work diagram (Figure 3.1). John decides he wants to learn the output of writing cost proposals. He makes an arrangement with Lee (with the cooperation of his manager) to co-write with the proposal writer an actual cost proposal. In this way, John is learning a new output to further his career development. Because the work diagram of the proposal writer specified the input, conditions, process, output, consequences, and feedback, John has a much better idea of what is needed to learn the cost proposal output. In helping John, Lee also has a clear idea of what is required. Again, by sharing work diagrams, workers can gain the clarity and insight they need to decide what to learn. They establish a cooperative sharing of "task practice" and gain the skill proficiency necessary for achievement. These skills help advance their skill base (and potentially, their monetary reward).

Similarly, management skills can be learned from other managers and colleagues. A common work language simply makes the planning and execution of career development opportunities so much easier to realize—and it can be done without a formalized, business-lead program.

Uses of the Work Language for Managers

Thus far we have seen how workers can use the Language of Work. There are also many uses for managers. In Chapter 1, Figure 1.3 outlines a number of these uses (see page 18). Some facilitate the management of workers (e.g., Task Assignment); others are helpful for personal management work (e.g., Work Planning). Those management functions that pertain to workers have been organized on a "line of use" from Job Description to Performance Review. Below each function is the suggested work application tool, although in some cases other tools may be used. The following descriptions are presented in the order shown in the diagram, beginning with Job Description.

- **Job Description**   *Tool: Work Table*

Many managers do not use job descriptions because they do not understand how job descriptions are properly constructed or how this aspect of management relates to business operations and business improvement. At the root of this problem, as well as so many other management problems, lies a fundamental lack of understanding work and what work entails. Figure 3.6, the description for Lee's job as a proposal writer, demonstrates how the Language of Work is used to help solve this basic problem. Clear and comprehensive job descriptions can be written. Note that the work table application tool was used to structure this job description (see Figure 3.5). Job descriptions can be written with or without an existing work table or work diagram. However, the presence of either is highly useful in developing a complete job description.

It is important to point out that the job accountabilities specified in a job description should match the outputs of an individual's work diagram; also, including a work diagram with the job description itself is appropriate. Moreover, a good narrative, such as the one found at the end of the sample job description, is an excellent addition to a job description, helping to interrelate the responsibilities and providing added detail about a job. The following list includes the outputs from Lee's work diagram (Figure 3.1) and their translation in the job description (Figure 3.6):

Outputs	*Accountabilities*
Cost Proposal	1. Develop cost proposals based on written proposal specifications and descriptions provided by clients.

71

JOB DESCRIPTION

TITLE: Proposal Writer   **BAND:** Technical

GROUP: Proposal Development   **JOB CODE:** HR 21

REPORTS TO: Proposal Development Manager

OBJECTIVE: Work on a team to develop well-written and cost-effective proposals in response to client needs for construction and engineering projects.

OUTPUTS: What results does this job produce?

1. Develop cost proposal based on written proposal specifications and descriptions provided by clients.
   – Cost proposal
2. Develop written proposals that reflect client needs and business capabilities to meet those needs.
   – Written proposal
3. Facilitate oral proposal development and practice to enhance proposed project team presentation to the potential client.
   – Oral presentation
   – Visuals
   – Presentation arrangements
4. Develop qualification statements in response to client requests.
   – Technical answers to specific client questions
   – Descriptions of services and related company project experience

INPUTS: What will you use to produce the results?
- Client RFPs (Requests for Proposal documentation)
- Proposal Development Manager direction, orientation to project, etc.
- Client Experience records (see files)
- Direct client contact—approval of manager

CONDITIONS: What things govern the use of the job resources and process used to produce results?
- Government regulations
- Company administrative policies and procedures manual
- Proposal Guidelines manual
- Knowledge of competition pricing, practices, and experience record— see files and in-house computer database for personnel

---

         Figure 3.6

PROCESS: How are the results produced in this job?

1. Analysis of the project starting with the RFP (or other) requirements
2. Allocation of team members to develop the proposal (sections)
3. First draft written
4. Review of first draft by a "Red Team"
5. Final copy and duplication
6. If required by client, oral presentation development and practice

CONSEQUENCES: What are the positive results you need to achieve?

- Winning the new project for the business
- Personal satisfaction
- Satisfaction of proposal manager

FEEDBACK: What information would help assure your achievement of the consequences and improve how you use the inputs, adhere to the conditions, complete the process, and achieve the outputs?

- Proposal Manager feedback during proposal development
- "We won the job!"
- Written or oral feedback (win or lose) from the client
- Planned schedule
- Red Team review

(see accompanying Job Description Narrative and Work Diagram)

JOB DESCRIPTION NARRATIVE: Proposal Writer

The proposal writer position is an important position that is at the heart of winning new business for the company. The major job accountabilities of this job include:

1. Develop cost proposal based on written proposal specifications and descriptions provided by clients.

2. Develop written proposals that reflect client needs and business capabilities to meet those needs.

3. Facilitate oral proposal development and practice to enhance proposed project team presentation to the potential client.

4. Develop qualification statements in response to client requests.

Figure 3.6 (continued)

(From p. 73)

To achieve these accountabilities, the proposal writer will typically work with a variety of technical and support positions, including engineers, managers, technicians, and clerical, training, and graphics/print personnel. Thus, the position requires not only solid writing skills but the capability to work closely and cooperatively with others.

Nature & Scope:

In a typical project, the proposal writer will receive direction from his or her proposal development manager regarding the need to respond to a client need (usually in a Request for Proposal) that the Sales and Marketing department has identified. An orientation session with the "proposal team" is held, during which the project scope is outlined, assignments made, and deadlines established. The proposal writer then analyzes the proposal needs, writes a draft version (working with others as needed), participates in a Red Team review, rewrites the proposal as needed, and assists in final duplication and printing. As a part of the process, the proposal writer also develops a cost proposal for their assigned area, although the proposal writer may be asked to assist in other costing areas of the proposal. The proposal writer may, in a similar way, be asked to write responses to qualification statements, as requested by clients. Finally, the proposal writer may also provide assistance to trainers to structure oral presentations for presenting the proposal to a client.

The scope of work may involve projects in the range of $80,000 to $3,000,000. The project team may range from as few as three to as many as 15 people. The opportunity for growth and personal satisfaction in winning new work for the company are particularly worth noting. Other details on this job are to be found in the detailed work elements found on page 1 and 2, and in the work diagram on the next page.

Required Attributes & Experience:

Excellent writing skills
Ability to work with others
Analytical skills

Figure 3.6 (concluded)

[NOTE: The work diagram for the proposal writer position as shown in Figure 3.1 would be included with the job description.]

Written Proposal	2. Develop written proposals that reflect client needs and business capabilities to meet those needs.
Oral Presentation	3. Facilitate oral proposal development and practice to enhance proposed project team presentation to the potential client.
Qualification Statements	4. Develop qualification statements in response to client requests.

The accountabilities are based directly on the outputs—these are, after all, what the position is supposed to achieve. In the execution of the job, the manager will assign individual tasks to achieve each of the accountabilities. Without a good job description, though, the manager cannot establish this link between accountabilities and task assignment. As will be seen in the following pages, good job descriptions are also essential for knowing what to facilitate, monitor, and measure, as well as for giving effective performance reviews. They can be the springboard to the successful fulfillment of other management functions, and are just one example of how the Language of Work links the seemingly unrelated job communication and implementation needs of managers.

• *Selection*   *Tool: Work Table*

Managers are at the forefront of selecting the workers that will best meet a business' needs through the execution of processes within a well-functioning work group. Therefore, managers not only have to know what the workers will do (their work diagrams), and can do (their skills and experience), but how they can handle what they are given (such as inputs, conditions), what motivates them (consequences), and how they will respond (feedback). All of this is made easier to remember to assess during a hiring/selection process when we use the Language of Work. Furthermore, a good job description is a helpful, if not a necessary, starting point for the selection process.

Basically, to do a selection the manager may use a work diagram of the job or a work table defining the various work elements of the job. These are far easier to refer to and use than a job description, but any one of the three will do. With these tools, the manager can assess the applicant's ability and experience regarding specific inputs, conditions, process, outputs, consequences, and feedback. The manager may also wish to assess additional skills associated with the work elements the applicant will be expected to execute on the job. The following is representative of many of the kinds of things a manager might look for.

75

Inputs
- What kinds of input (e.g., client needs) has this person used that are similar to the inputs the person will be using in our company?

Conditions
- What awareness does this person have of government regulations and our competition that will affect the person's use of inputs and process?

Process
- How much training or retraining will be required for the individual to learn our processes?

Outputs
- What quality standards does the individual apply to the output?

Consequences
- What attention does the applicant pay to satisfaction of internal clients?

Feedback
- What kinds of specific help does the applicant seek on his or her own to do the best job of processing?

• **Task Assignment**   *Tool: Talking Work*

By definition, tasks are the individual activities that workers engage in to achieve their specific accountabilities (outputs). One of the major difficulties managers at all levels seem to have is communicating, monitoring, facilitating, and providing feedback relative to individual and team task assignments. When a manager and worker are operating from a common work language, however, many of these communication difficulties are minimized or disappear. The manager can, for example, create a dialogue scenario with workers as follows:

- "This is an output (accountability) you are responsible for, and in relation to that output, here is a task that I want you to complete."

- "To do this task, you will need the following inputs. . . ."

- "As you are aware, there are certain conditions the company, our client, and the government impose on the output, including . . . . You will need to be particularly aware of . . ."

- "The process used to do this task involves the following steps, during which you will interact with the following people, departments, and outside resources, as well as . . ."

- "Along the way, I and the following individuals will provide you feedback in the completion of this task . . . . What further feedback would you like me to provide as your manager?"

- "The consequences of doing this task are the following . . . ."

Here is an example of the above scenario applied to one of the sample jobs, that of Monica, the trainer. In this case, the task assignment uses a simple talking-work application tool.

"Monica, you are to produce a new training program **[her output]** in the form of a computer-based interactive simulation of our new press, the Mark V. To do this, you will need to work with Bill Sanders, who is chief operator of the press, Warren Williams of New Press Technologies, and Wanda Phillips, our internal computer-operations manager. You will probably have to bring others in as well. Your budget for the project is $40,000. This is based on the response to a needs assessment study that was completed by the Press Operations groups. **[These are various inputs.]**

"You will have to follow the guidelines for computer instruction that we established in our Training Design manual, as well as follow the technical specifications of the manufacturer. **[These are some of the conditions.]** Of course, you will use our Instructional Technology approach as your process—as you have done before and as emphasized in the recent refresher course. **[This is the process.]**

"You should plan to measure satisfaction with the course by a satisfaction survey. You will also conduct a validation testing program as part of the Instructional Technology process. We anticipate that technicians should be able to come up to speed on the press within six months. Proficiency standards will have to be defined and applied. There are areas of growth for you as well, in added experience in computer-aided instruction. **[These are consequences.]**

"Finally, as you proceed with the analysis, development, tryout, and measurement of this training program, I would like you to check with me at a minimum before and after completing each of these major steps. I would like you to provide me with a series of checkpoint dates. At what other points in the process of development do you think you and I should talk?" **[These are forms of feedback.]**

A task assignment such as this would naturally contain more dialogue between manager and worker than given here, and not sound so mechanical (although some workers would appreciate such a mechanical approach because it provides complete information). Yet, this sample does demonstrate that a complete and organized approach to task assignments will benefit both worker and manager. When managers combine the use of the work language with the right tone of dealing with another person and then follow up with encouragement, workers are very responsive and their efforts at improvement increase. Equipped with clear task assignments, workers can concentrate on *their work*, and managers can help them improve performance, rather than having to waste time trying to compensate for insufficient forms of communication.

• Facilitating Work   *Tool: Talking Work*

Managers have long pondered the dilemma of how much control they should exercise in the workplace: When should they *supervise* workers? When should they *do the work* for the workers? Today, because so many managers view work in a limited way, as only process, they typically respond to this dilemma by engaging in the process themselves. This merely sets off a chain reaction of further problems, for, as we have seen, work actually comprises *six* elements, not just the single element of process.

To constructively deal with the problem of control and *facilitate* the accomplishment of work, managers must recognize the complete meaning of work. The Language of Work helps managers understand what is involved in facilitation and when control measures, such as engaging in the process, must be taken. When equipped with this language, managers approach facilitation in the following ways:

For Inputs:
  – Check the reliability, quality, and other features of inputs needed to produce quality outputs.

For Conditions:
  – Inform workers of conditions.
  – Reinforce workers for the use or adherence to conditions.

For Processes:
  – Attend to the worker's use of approved processes.
  – Listen and act on suggested improvements to processes.
  – Only perform the work process when needed (when managers do the work, the workers are not performing adequately).

For Outputs:
  – Provide feedback when the output is complete.
  – Provide and listen to suggestions for making outputs better.

For Consequences:
  − Reinforce consequences.
  − Work for the trust of the workers.

For Feedback:
  − Seek feedback rather than wait for it.
  − Plan for feedback at predetermined checkpoints.
  − Measure, rather than guess at, client satisfaction.

• **Reinforcement**   *Tool: Talking Work*

Positive reinforcement is how we reward individuals, teams, and various work groups for what they do. Understanding when and where to give reinforcement is one of the many advantages of using the work language that managers need to pay attention to. Simply put, if managers don't adequately provide the right amount and kinds of reinforcement, individuals are not as apt to repeat work done well or learn how to avoid poor performance. The two main areas that afford opportunities for reinforcement are consequences and feedback, though all six work elements greatly benefit from reinforcement.

Positive feedback should be included among the many consequences of work. Knowing that a job has been done well is a good feeling for the ones who produce the output. And they should be told so and not be taken for granted or, worse yet, completely ignored. It is a major responsibility of a manager to be the one who recognizes and gives this reinforcement.

Feedback, by its very nature, invites reinforcement. Feedback should provide clarifying information during processing and after completion of an output. It should also make individuals feel good about what they have done. This distinction is simply a matter of not only telling the worker or manager that the job was finished, but also recognizing that it was done well. The following is an example of reinforcement provided to Monica by her manager. As with the sample task assignment, actual reinforcement would not sound so mechanical; the purpose of the sample is to demonstrate the general nature and elements of work that need reinforcement.

"Monica, your work on the new training program for the computer-based interactive simulation of our new press, the Mark V, was simply outstanding. Bill Sanders, Warren Williams, and Wanda Phillips all told me that the program is really doing the job. I am delighted that you were able to work with them so well. And you stayed right within budget! **[The manager has reinforced the quality of the output and Monica's use of the various inputs.]**

"I want to congratulate you on using the Instructional Technology approach, and you obviously followed the guidelines for computer instruction that we established in our Training Design manual, as well as the technical specifications of the manufacturer. **[These reinforce Monica's adherence to the process and the conditions.]**

"Furthermore, I note that the satisfaction surveys completed by the press operators who received the training indicate a high level of satisfaction with the training they received. Moreover, they have been able to come up to speed on the press within six months.

"I would like to talk to you about what areas of growth you felt you achieved by working on this project, as well as any added experience you gained in computer-aided instruction. **[These are reinforcement of consequences.]**

"Finally, I want to thank you for staying in touch with me during each major step of the process. Do you think there were times when I could have done more for or with you?" **[These reinforce feedback.]**

• **Quality Measurement**   *Tools: Work Diagram*
                                           Talking Work

It is, of course, one of the principal tasks of a manager to assess work for the specific purpose of improving quality. Nowhere is quality improvement more directly needed on an ongoing basis than with the individual or team. The use of a work language, particularly in the form of work diagrams, identifies areas of potential improvement and provides the key to actual improvement. Results can occur in several ways.

As we have seen, the mere process of an individual defining the work elements and constructing a work diagram (in agreement with management) leads to role clarification. This in itself helps the individual improve quality to some degree. When the role clarification is approached as a task shared between individual and manager, there is also improved communication—another quality improvement. However, by far the greatest improvement in quality can be achieved by other uses of work diagrams.

In the discussion of the uses of the work language for workers, we learned that individuals can measure efficiency through the consequences of, and feedback on, their accountabilities (i.e., outputs). Managers can work with workers to develop and implement performance measures such as these and to talk about quality improvement. For example, when I was responsible for developing, implementing, and managing a TQM process, my accountabilities included, among others, the following:

1. Implement a TQM orientation for employees.

2. Develop training programs in TQM techniques.

3. Facilitate Quality Team efforts in implementing the TQM process.

My manager and I developed and implemented, as a cooperative effort, performance measures for these accountabilities; for example, a satisfaction survey that was given to workers who completed TQM orientation sessions (the first accountability) and manager observation of my efforts to facilitate team meetings (the third accountability). Through the survey results and the feedback provided by my manager after the team meetings, I learned how to improve the quality of my output in these areas.

Since my outputs were measured on an ongoing basis as the work was done, my manager and I were able to have in-depth and meaningful discussions on quality improvement—discussions between manager and worker that were more effective than the usual annual or semi-annual performance review. In discussing the first accountability, for example, we covered ground on what specific inputs affected the process (e.g., teaching techniques), what process improvements could be made, and so on, including consequences, feedback, and conditions. This is true quality improvement on an ongoing basis—and this method, based on the work language, can be used in any business.

- **Performance Review**   *Tool: Talking Work*

There is probably no single aspect of management skill that befuddles a manager more than reviewing a worker's performance. Managers just don't seem to know how to do it, and avoid it at all cost. I can personally recall a manager or two who simply announced to me (on the fly), "You're doing a good job!" What kind of performance evaluation is that? And yet, if a worker is ever to grow and do better on the job, managers have to do adequate performance reviews. From my own experience, I know the Language of Work definitely helps in this regard. The following is an approach to performance review that I have successfully used many times in my role as a facilitator—*facilitator* being a term I much prefer to *manager, supervisor,* and *administrator.*

First, a good performance review has one basic prerequisite: a good job description. As we have seen, a good job description includes an initial description, in which the outputs are defined, and a subsequent description narrative, in which the outputs are detailed and referred to as accountabilities. (A work diagram is also provided.) Most jobs have about five to seven major accountabilities. Here is an accountability that I had as the director of a TQM process:

"Measure the success of a total quality management process in terms of internal client satisfaction."

When it comes time for a performance review, the worker and the manager write a description of the extent to which each accountability has been achieved. (Remember, the accountabilities are also used to give task assignments.) It is important to stress that these descriptions are not general illustrations of the entire job or of major tasks completed, as is the case in most performance reviews; rather, they focus on the specific job accountabilities. Once these descriptions are completed, a detailed discussion follows, centering on the work diagram or work table for the worker's job. For example, for the accountability in the paragraph above, the written descriptions and face-to-face talk between the worker and the manager would focus on answering these kinds of questions:

For Outputs:
  – Were the outputs delivered to specifications on time and within budget?

For Inputs:
  – What sorts of inputs were provided, or not provided, to do your individual tasks in achieving this accountability?

For Conditions:
  – What conditions changed or were not clear, thus affecting the successful completion of your tasks? Were means provided to compensate for these changes?

For Process:
  – What breakdowns, if any, occurred in the process, thus affecting the achievement of outputs?
  – What interrelationships with other departments affected the processing of tasks?

For Consequences:
  – Were standards of internal/external client satisfaction achieved from the outputs?
  – Where output standards were not achieved was the client eventually given satisfaction?
  – How do you feel about what you personally achieved in this accountability?
  – What would you like me, as your supervisor, to do to assure your continued success and growth?

For Feedback:
- As your facilitator, did I provide progressive stages of feedback that helped you complete your tasks?
- Did others in the process provide you with the kind of feedback needed to complete your task adequately in terms of quality, cost, and timing?

When the six elements of the work language are used, the exchange between worker and manager is much more complete in terms of what work is and how it can be achieved. The work-language structure of a performance review affords more opportunity for growth, for learning what went right and what went wrong, and for determining how the job can be done better in the future.

• Work Needs Assessment   *Tool: Work Matrix*

Needs assessment is the activity of determining when work requirements need to change. Many of these, of course, should come out of the planned activities of the business, including business planning and quality improvement processes. But many also fall on the shoulders of the astute manager, who must determine these changes within his or her own work group and processes. Work changes are not necessarily big changes; indeed, they are often those little things that help "tweak" the system. The Language of Work can help a manager find the needed ones.

In the field of Human Performance Technology, needs are defined as the difference between "what is" and "what should be." In translating this to the Language of Work, we can set up a work matrix that provides managers with a useful work analysis tool for determining what aspects of work can be improved. For example, suppose Lee's manager, in an ongoing assessment of the overall process used for proposal development, determines that a change seems to be needed in the way information about potential clients is gathered and accessed; his proposal writers are simply spending an inordinate amount of time gathering strategically useful background information on the client for which they are writing a proposal. Using a work matrix approach to defining this need, the manager produces the analysis shown in Figure 3.7 (See page 84).

As you review the Work Needs Assessment Matrix (Figure 3.7), note that it is composed of two columns where the manager lists "What Exists" for all six elements of the work being analyzed, and then lists "What Should Exist" for each element. A goal statement of the need is given at the top of page. When complete, the matrix lists the specific needs. For example, we see that certain new input needs have been identified, no change in the conditions, some desirable changes in the process, an improved output, further consequences that should result, and no change in the feedback. What the matrix of work needs suggests to this manager is that a change from a "file drawer" to a computerized quick-access system of current and new client information is needed. The matrix also indicates the need for a system that will periodically purge old information and incorporate additional client information sources.

WORK NEEDS ASSESSMENT MATRIX

NEED TO ANALYZE: Better client information for proposal development activities.

	WHAT EXISTS	**WHAT SHOULD EXIST**
INPUTS	• Trade journals • Annual reports • Previous employees • Joint venture proposals • Phone inquiry • Business Development/ Sales Mgr.	Same + • Trade associations • Field personnel
CONDITIONS	• Freedom of Information Act	Same
PROCESS	• Client Experience files • Personal contacts	• Quicker access • More complete information • Up-to-date information • Periodic purging
OUTPUT	• Client Profile Sheet	• Improved client profile

CONSEQUENCES	• Specific client response
	  in proposal
	• Competition
	• Increased chance of
	  winning the job
		Same +
		• Relevant pricing
		• Political sensitivity
		• Client "hot buttons"

FEEDBACK	• New employee client profile of prior company • Win ratio • Sales Manager visit • Post-presentation assessment • Annual client eval. retreat	Same

Figure 3.7

• Work Planning   *Tool: Work Table*

Work planning is one of the major roles of a manager. Planning must assure that the work is well thought out in light of all that has to be accomplished with the resources and budget available, and according to standards and time limits. How can the Language of Work be useful in helping the manager plan work?

One example is shown in Figure 3.8. This is only one way to plan work; the work table can be modified to include other planning information that needs to be shown. In this case, dates of completion and the responsible person are shown for an activity in Lee's work area: writing a specific client proposal. This information, planned by Lee's manager, will assist Lee and other team members in knowing when various aspects of the work need to be planned for completion. Note carefully that nearly all the information from the definition of Lee's job in his work diagram (Figure 3.1) is included in the work plan. Later, when you see the process work diagram for the proposal development work group, you will see an even closer relationship to the information in this work plan.

• **Work Analysis**   *Tool: Work Diagram*

Work analysis, for the purposes of this book, comprises those activities related to analyzing individual jobs, processes, and work groups using the Language of Work approach described earlier in this chapter. This means using performance questions to measure and improve work and constructing work diagrams. Details on these two methods are provided in subsequent chapters.

Uses of the Work Language for Teams

The Language of Work is well suited for team use, particularly when team members exhibit difficulty working with one another. Using the same work language can go a long way in improving the team effort. For an example, see Team Accountabilities, Figure 3.9, for just a few ways

• **Team Role Clarification**   *Tool: Work Table*

As is true with individuals, a common work language can be very successfully applied to helping a new team establish role definition or clarification. For example, in Figure 3.9, you find the accountabilities for a team known from a TQM process as an "improvement team." An improvement team takes a quality improvement idea (need) and formulates a solution, tries it out, measures its success, and makes revisions in the solution as needed. The role of this team was determined and clarified by defining the accountabilities in Figure 3.9. The accountabilities themselves were determined by first defining the outputs the improvement team would produce. The outputs included:

1. Solutions to quality improvement points

2. Measured quality improvements

3. Assigned team roles

WORK PLANNING WORK TABLE

Client: GTO   **Project: Written & Cost Proposal, Presentation**

	TIME (Due Date)	RESPONSIBLE PERSON
INPUTS		
RFP	September 21	Proposal Dev. Manager
Proposal Mgr. guidelines	September 25	Proposal Dev. Manager
Client Experience files	September 26	Archives Assistant
Contact client	October 29	Project Manager
CONDITIONS		
Company policies	September 25	Proposal Dev. Manager
Government regs.	September 25	Proposal Dev. Manager
Proposal guidelines	September 25	Proposal Dev. Manager
Competition report	September 25	Sales and Marketing
PROCESS		
1. RFP analysis	September 26	Proposal Dev. Manager
2. Development team / Resources allocation	October 1	Proposal Dev. Manager
3. First draft	October 28	Proposal Writer
4. Red Team review	November 1	Red Team Manager
5. Final copy & duplication	November 10 November 12	Proposal Writer Print Shop
6. Oral presentation	November 28	Trainer
OUTPUTS		
Written proposal	Due November 16	Proposal Dev. Manager
Cost proposal	Due November 16	Proposal Dev. Manager
Oral presentation	Tentatively, Dec. 1	Trainer
CONSEQUENCES		
"Winning the Job"	Dec. 1 - Award date	
FEEDBACK		
Proposal plan	September 26	Proposal Dev. Manager
1st draft review	October 30	Proposal Dev. Manager
Red Team evaluation	November 3	Red Team Manager
Final draft review	November 7	Proposal Dev. Manager
Publication review	November 13	Proposal Dev. Manager
Oral presentation review	November 26	Trainer

Figure 3.8

TEAM ACCOUNTABILITIES (OUTPUTS)

1. Use systematic processes to solve quality improvement points (QIPs) assigned by a Quality Team.

2. Measure the effectiveness and efficiency (includes time and economic results) of the QIP solution, and report the results on WD #6, QIP Implementation Form.

3. Elect membership roles for members of your Improvement Team commensurate with the description provided in the TQM Handbook.

4. Regularly inform, in writing, your Quality Team as to the progress of your team in solving the QIP you have been assigned.

5. Identify, describe on WD #4 (QIP Source Form), and send to the Quality Team any suggested QIPs that result from work the Improvement Team does in solving its assigned QIP.

6. Provide recognition to Improvement Team members.

7. Solicit training opportunities that are needed to meet your need to solve and measure QIPs.

PROMOTE:

1. An atmosphere in which all associates know that the team responds to, and cares about, their suggestions

2. Communication that is open and honest on all matters

3. Recognition for individual and team work

4. Fairness in your deliberations

5. A team approach versus a management mandate

6. Measurement of results

Figure 3.9

4. Informed management and others

5. Suggested improvements from team work

6. Recognition of individuals for quality efforts

7. Training programs for team skill-building implemented

Following the definition of outputs (and translation into team accountabilities), we back up in the Language of Work and define the specific inputs, conditions, process, consequences, and feedback the team will need to perform in accomplishing each output. For example, the sixth output listed above would need the work elements defined in the following work table:

Improvement Team Role Definition

Output 1	• **Recognition of individuals for quality efforts**
Inputs	• **Recommendation solicited** • **Survey clients** • **Evaluation of solutions**
Conditions	• **Quality Standards criteria** • **Systems Approach used** • **Awards policy**
Process	• **Nominations** • **Judging against criteria** • **Selection** • **Reward/Award**
Consequences	• **Recipients feel recognized/good** • **Work groups are inspired to contribute** • **More quality needs received**
Feedback	• **Recipient's reaction** • **Attitude survey of group** • **Informal observations**

Defining the six elements of work for each team output or accountability provides clarification of the improvement team's role as a team. This clarification will be quite useful to individual team members and the team as a whole in doing their work and explaining their work to others (e.g., management, those they will need information from, and so forth). The work elements are best defined by the improvement team itself during a group discussion. This enhances the buy-in to their actual use because the team determines what makes up inputs, conditions, process, consequences, and needed feedback. In using the work table application tool, they carefully define and clarify their role as a team. And the group discussion of the definition helps build teamwork through the active involvement and buy-in of everyone on the team.

• *Individual Responsibility*   *Tool: Work Table*

Individual responsibility on a team will vary depending on the kind of team. For example, the team in Figure 3.9 is basically a problem-solving team. Other teams have different purposes, such as data collection, policy advisorship, implementation support, and measurement. Roles for specific members of the team may also be designated. For example, there might be a team leader, organizer, implementer, and recorder. Whatever the individual's role, a work table will be useful to the individual and to the team. For an example, let's look at the role of the team leader.

Assume you are assigned the role of a team leader. You and others on the team develop on the board a work table for the team leader position and discuss it so that there is consensus on the definition of your role. Here are some accountabilities for your team leader role:

- Lead team discussion and problem solving

- Communicate with improvement team

- Complete and transmit all working documents to TQM administrator

- Set and follow meeting agenda

- Assign other roles to team members

- Assess team progress

These are, as you know, derived from first defining the team leader's outputs. This means we can apply the work language to the team leader's role and define his or her corresponding inputs, conditions, process, consequences, and feedback to complete and support the outputs. Examples of these work elements for the team leader are as follows:

Improvement Team Role Definition
Team Leader

Outputs	• Team discussions • Problems solved • Communication documentation • Meeting agenda • Assign team roles • Measure team progress
Inputs	• Problems • Surveys • Assessments
Conditions	• TQM procedures and standards • Management support • Company policies
Process	• Meetings • Problem solving • Measurements
Consequences	• Problems solved • Needs realized • Personal growth
Feedback	• Client satisfaction surveys • Management assessments • Measurement of solutions

Since the work table will be developed with the other team members and consensus reached on the role of the team leader, we can expect this role to be clear for all members of the team. In a similar way, the team will also want to define each team member's individual role (e.g., organizer, implementer, recorder) and the team members' relationships to one another in the following areas:

- Mutual outputs, process, interactions

- When and where feedback is needed to keep
  one another informed

Your team may even want to go so far as to define relationships with others outside the team to assure other effective and efficient role relationships.

- **Problem Solving**   *Tool: Work Matrix*

Unfortunately a team can be one of the most inefficient of organizations. This is especially true when it comes to the area of problem solving. Typically, teams do the best they can do by holding discussions on how they would solve a problem. Generally speaking, "how they would solve a problem" is more an open discussion than true problem solving. Here again is a perfect opportunity to use the work language—and in a unique and highly effective way through the work matrix application tool. In Chapter 6 you will be provided a description of "knowledge processes." You are encouraged to use the work matrix suggested there for team processing as it relates to solving problems.

- **Team Measurement**   *Tool: Work Plan*

Review again in Figure 3.9 the list of accountabilities for an improvement team. On careful inspection, you may notice that each of these accountabilities can be measured. We could, for instance, construct and conduct a survey of users (employees) of the TQM process to see how they perceive the effectiveness of an improvement team in solving a particular problem of concern to the users. Since the list of accountabilities represents the output of the team, we could ask team members to evaluate how well each output was achieved. For example: Did they feel that they received recognition (output 6)? Did they receive training (output 7)? In a similar way, each output or accountability can be measured and quality improvement can be undertaken. This quality improvement of a team follows the same procedure that was previously described for individual improvement.

BENEFITS OF USING THE LANGUAGE OF WORK ON THE INDIVIDUAL LEVEL

This chapter has underscored a vitally important point: that the opportunity for significant business improvement is no more apparent than on the individual level, in the contributions of individual workers, managers, and teams—especially contributions achieved through self-motivated efforts. To make these contributions, however, individuals need more than personal initiative; they need analytical and communication tools that they can use on their own and in working with others, especially management.

Much of the improvement can be made possible if individuals know how to look at their own work in a performance-oriented, systematic way. The Language of Work provides them with such a way, helping them communicate with one another in their common effort to understand and execute their work and to make it better. In turn, this same language is useful for teams. Then, when used with the entire business unit by various work groups engaged in various processes, the work language becomes a very strong force in holding all aspects of a business together and making it better and better. This common work language becomes the strongest glue that holds and strengthens the business.

By using a common work language, individual workers can expect these benefits:

- Increased role clarification—clear understanding of what they are expected to do with what inputs, under what conditions, through what process, for what consequences

- Facilitation that provides effective feedback

- Enhancement in their role relationships with other workers, so that they can mutually help one another, thus helping the business as a whole

- A means to measure personal effectiveness and efficiency and to make improvements without having to rely on management

- Self-directed career development

For the manager facilitating the work force, management functions are enhanced by using work application tools in such areas as:

- Task assignments

- Performance reviews

- Job descriptions utilization

- Appropriate use of feedback

- Providing reinforcement

- Quality improvement efforts

- Facilitating work

For teams of workers, benefits accrue in:

- Team role clarification

- Individual responsibilities

- Problem solving

- Measurement of team effectiveness

Having introduced the Language of Work into various businesses, I recommend that when installing the Language of Work into your company, you first give particular attention to the information that has been introduced in this chapter. By doing so, you will give all workers and managers an opportunity to use the Language of Work on themselves, to see its value directly and get used to "speaking" the language in many ways. Then, having experienced the language yourself and with others for a period of six to nine months, you will be in a position to see how the language can be used in the specific context of the business unit, processes, and work groups. We will begin the broader use of the Language of Work with the business unit in the next chapter.

CHAPTER 4

APPLYING THE LANGUAGE OF WORK TO THE BUSINESS UNIT

This book has now started you on the road to learning the Language of Work by helping you apply the language to yourself as an individual in the Business Sphere. Yet, although it is important to begin learning and practicing the language at the Individual level, it is recommended that you begin your actual analysis of a business at the Business Unit level. Why? Because businesses are in business first and foremost to meet their goals; they must know where they are headed before they can decide where individuals fit best into the workplace. This is a classic case of DEFINE AUSTRALIA FIRST. The overall outputs of the business, represented by the Business Unit level, need to be defined and known by all who are part of the business before the more detailed relationships between work groups (Chapter 5), processes (Chapter 6), and individuals (Chapter 3) are analyzed.

ORDER OF ANALYSIS IN THE BUSINESS SPHERE

To understand how important it is to analyze the four levels of business in the proper order, consider the following. Anyone involved in business has most likely seen management reverse the order in which to go about improving the efficiency and effectiveness of a business—and that this "reverse order of analysis," as we might call it, did not produce the kinds of results anticipated. Some instances of "reverse-order analysis" include:

- Analyzing processes and fixing them before determining if there is anything wrong with the primary outputs of the business

- Analyzing what is wrong with individuals (workers, managers, or teams) without having determined if there is something wrong with the processes they employ

- Analyzing and reorganizing a work group before seeing if the right process and individuals are present to achieve the defined business outputs

- Hiring individuals before defining and communicating what processes they will be expected to employ to achieve the primary outputs of the business

In general, reverse-order analysis causes more problems than it solves. Quite simply, it makes no sense—yet businesses often fail to recognize this fact.

For example, it is clearly senseless to analyze processes before deciding if the overall output is satisfactory, and yet this is often done by managers on their own or, in some instances, in the implementation of total quality management. Recently an executive on an airline flight lamented to me about having to define all the processes to meet the ISO 9000 (the European) standards in his company. The problem was not that he objected to defining the processes, nor did he object to ISO 9000 standards; rather, he objected to the processes being defined before the overall goals (outputs) first had been defined, measured, and analyzed. The business was analyzing the processes to meet a standard rather than to *improve* the processes relative to specific outputs that needed fixing. They were also doing a process analysis that was void of any tangible evidence of client dissatisfaction with the outputs produced from those processes.

In another case, a CEO of a large corporation decided to reorganize the work groups without first investigating whether there was any problem with the processes or the individuals who produced the primary outputs. He knew there was something wrong with achievement of the business goals (their outputs), and he assumed the problem was with the work groups (the organization structure/chart). In this case, he needed to measure the primary outputs, then look at the processes and individuals, and last, the organization chart. What he was doing, in a sense, was applying his financial language, rather than an understanding of a work language, to an existing problem and how best to solve it. In this instance, I recall asking the CEO to please agree to look at process before reorganizing the work groups. The CEO agreed that this would make sense and that he would guard against it the next time change was needed in the corporation. Alas, within six months he had reorganized the work groups again without having looked at the processes. Does this sound familiar? If you have ever been reorganized, chances are you have experienced a reverse-order analysis of the Business Sphere.

In the work analysis approach emphasized in this book, the four levels of business are analyzed in a logical sequence. The unique position and interrelationships among the levels are fully recognized, as well as their interdependencies. The analysis of one is undertaken and measured as the basis of knowledge and business improvement prior to analysis of other levels. Certainly, an analysis using the work language can be done at any business level in any order, but there is a preferred order that builds each business level on the next level. The reasons for a preferred order of analysis may be summarized by posing and answering the following questions.

- Why not start with the Individual level?

Analyzing the Individual level prior to analyzing the business unit, processes, or work groups would not be logical. How can we determine what the individual's work diagram should be until we know the overall processes that govern what the individual will do? These processes in turn are part of an overall business unit's set of goals and strategies to achieve primary business outputs.

- Why not start with the Process level?

To start with the Process level without consideration of where the business unit is headed would not make sense. Remember that we must DEFINE AUSTRALIA FIRST (determine our destination) before deciding on process (how to get there).

- Why not start with the Work Group level?

To start with the work groups would be senseless without our first knowing the business unit's major outputs and analyzing to see if these outputs are being achieved. Also, since work groups generally represent the way the business is organized and communicates, it does not make sense to *organize* for work until we know what work outputs the business is going to produce and what process and individuals are required to get there. Work groups are really the last level in business to determine or analyze—a consideration that runs quite contrary to much of today's business practice, in which work groups are often the first thing to be changed in a business.

For these and many other reasons, we should begin our task of improving the business with a careful analysis of the overall business unit first. Then we can analyze, in order, the processes, individuals, and work groups. Why this order?

First: Business Unit Analysis defines and measures the overall business outputs.

Second: Process Analysis defines and measures the processes needed to achieve the business outputs.

Third: Individual analysis defines, selects, and measures the individuals needed to use the processes to achieve the business outputs.

| **Fourth:** | Work Group Analysis defines and measures the best organization and communication of individuals to use processes to produce the business outputs. |

DO NOT REVERSE or REORDER this sequence, or you will risk fixing what does not need fixing or reorganizing work groups when it is not the best solution to improve the business.

DEFINING AND MEASURING THE BUSINESS UNIT

One of the first things you will discover about defining and measuring the business unit, or conducting Business Unit Analysis, is that many people in business initially find it difficult to do an analysis. This is one reason why introducing the Language of Work at the Individual level is so important. This initial difficulty points out a major problem in business: Many workers and managers (including executives) have no idea how to analyze and improve themselves or their business. Learning to define the business is therefore all the more crucial. As they work on the definition, discovering unknown relationships, lack of emphasis on consequences and feedback, poorly defined processes, and the like, they may wonder how business was ever run with any degree of effectiveness and efficiency in the first place. Through their analysis they will head up the path to real improvements.

When we do Business Unit Analysis, we discover and clarify the important contribution of, and relationship between, work groups that are involved in using the business outputs. In the absence of such analysis, management often overlooks the full potential of these work groups and their value to the overall success of a business. I have witnessed this problem in several businesses. For instance, in one company the training work group was capable of aiding in the improvement of business operations through the utilization of a variety of interventions, but instead it was used to provide "occasional" training at the discretion of virtually any manager. There were no plans to support improving, through training, the processes that produced primary outputs; for example, training marketing personnel in giving better presentations, writing proposals, and so forth—training that added value to the business unit.

The root of this problem can be traced to a limited perception of work groups, which itself is a result of a limited perspective on work. Work groups are often viewed as mere symbols of routine activity or temporary fixes, rather than as excellent resources for improving the short - or long-term needs of the business unit. The failure lies not in the manager's unwillingness to make the business better as much as it does in the lack of a way for the manager to look at work, analyze it, and make it better. Business Unit Analysis, along with other levels of analysis that will be introduced later, goes a long way in helping both manager and worker broaden and deepen their perception, thus improving their jobs and their business.

BUSINESS UNIT ANALYSIS: USING THE WORK DIAGRAM APPLICATION TOOL

In Chapter 3 you were introduced to a work application tool known as the work diagram. You diagrammed your own job, applying this tool on the Individual level, and reviewed the work diagrams for our sample workers—Lee, John, and Monica. The work diagram can be used effectively throughout the other levels of a business as well—processes, work groups, and the business unit. Thus, the Language of Work, a *universal* work language, helps us define all the levels of a business.

The value of diagramming the business unit is not just that it gives us a common model for viewing the entire business. More fundamental is that diagramming gives us a conceptual model in a graphic form—we can look at a work diagram, discuss its meaning, and use it to arrive at consensus on the definition of the business unit. The layout of a diagram gives us a comprehensive view of the six work elements, their specific content, and how they interrelate with one another. For example, we can easily see all the inputs and outputs of a business and how the process flows (depicted by arrows) to complete the outputs, using the inputs. Other application tools, such as work tables and work plans, rely mostly on words and, therefore, do not provide such a concrete and easily understood picture of the business. They can be used to define the business unit and will be useful for certain other needs (i.e., business plans) in defining the business, but the work diagram is by far the best application tool for defining the business unit and other levels of the Business Sphere.

We will now see how the work diagram is specifically developed and used in analyzing the business unit.

Developing the Business-Unit Work Diagram: A Sample Case

As a practical matter, the definition of the business unit should be undertaken by a team of executives and workers, whose task will be to define an initial draft of a work diagram for the business unit. They will then share this draft with others for refinement and "buy-in." An orientation to the Language of Work will be needed as an initial step. The following approach is highly recommended. First, instruct each individual on the team to construct a work diagram for his or her own job (yes, even executives can diagram their own job). This helps demonstrate that each individual knows how to diagram using the Language of Work. Then, introduce representative examples of various business-unit work diagrams, such as the example found in this chapter.

As we have seen in Chapters 1 and 3, a work diagram involves the analysis of inputs, conditions, process, outputs, consequences, and feedback. Figure 4.1 is a typical work diagram for a business unit (see page 101). The example is an engineering business unit that can represent either an entire corporate entity or a significant business unit, such as a major division, of a large corporation. The latter "division" is a business unit because it produces primary for-profit services and products for external clients, thus functioning as a "profit center."

If you compare Figure 4.1, the work diagram for a business unit, to Figures 3.1 through 3.3, work diagrams for individuals, you can see the similarity in their structure. All six work elements appear in the same position, with outputs on the right, inputs on the left, conditions in the upper left corner (labeled "Doing Business Influences"), process in the middle between inputs and outputs, consequences (not listed on the business-unit work diagram itself) on the far right, and feedback represented by arrows. The only difference is that the process is specified in some detail for the business unit but not at all for the individual.

Figure 4.1 is a useful example of a work diagram for a business unit not only because it is a good representation of such work diagrams in general, but also because it is an actual diagram used by a business. The business' work is oriented towards engineering and project management, as is often the case in design and construction businesses. The following scenario describes how the sample work diagram was formulated by a team of executives, managers, and others who were given the assignment of analyzing and improving a business unit using the work language approach.

Case: Engineering Business
Case Description:

An area office of a large environmental services corporation provides engineering services to local government and private businesses related to clean-up and preventative measures to meet federal environmental regulations. Some months ago the corporation adopted the Language of Work approach in order to improve everyday work communication and as the foundation for their quality improvement program. Through the corporation, workers and managers received training in the Language of Work, and they have been using it on an ongoing basis for a variety of work functions, such as writing job descriptions, selecting new hires, giving task assignments, doing period performance reviews, planning work, solving problems, conducting team activities, and the like. Thus, workers and managers generally know the Language of Work and have used it on themselves and with others in the corporation. Now the various business offices, of which there are about 40 scattered throughout the United States, are going to define their individual business units using the Language of Work approach. The vice-president of each local business-unit office has selected an initial team of managers and workers from within this business to draft a version of the business-unit work diagram.

The team includes three direct reports representing engineering, project management, and office management. These managers are joined by three representatives from a cross section of the business: an accountant, a marketing and sales representative, and the head of quality assurance. In this way the team is more than

100

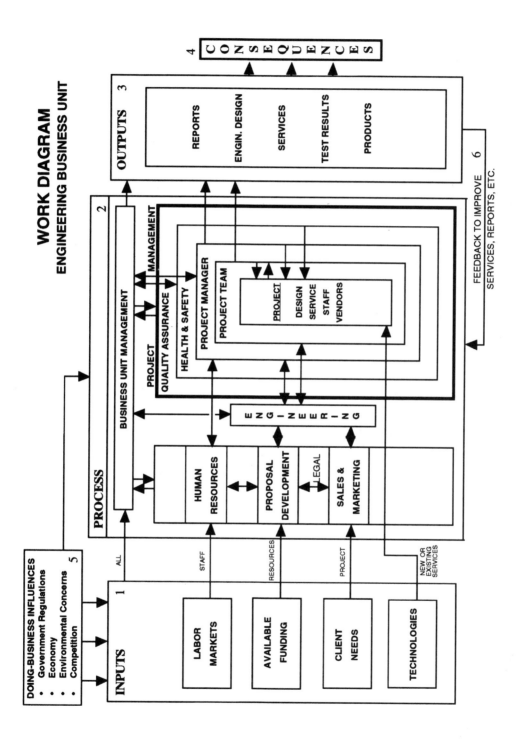

Figure 4.1

simply a management team; it represents a cross section of everyone in the business unit, including nonsupervisory workers. A facilitator from the corporate quality-improvement work group has arrived at the office and is prepared to help guide the local office team in developing their business-unit work diagram. The following nine steps are taken.

Step 1: Orientation

The facilitator conducts an orientation to what the team will be doing, how it is to do its work, and how it is to be organized. Since everyone has used the Language of Work for the past six months, there is general agreement on the meaning of outputs, inputs, conditions, process, consequences, and feedback. The goal of their task is to define a work diagram that depicts their business unit, to confirm their definition of the business with others in the business unit, and then, having reached consensus, to measure the business and make needed changes that will produce quality improvements in the business.

Step 2: Define Outputs

The team, led by the vice-president of the business unit and aided by the corporate facilitator when needed, begins by defining the major outputs of the business. These are listed on flip-chart paper by one member of the team designated as the recorder. The outputs, shown below, include reports, engineering designs, services, tests, and products. Thus, this business unit is predominately a service business, although there is some product. These are fairly typical outputs of engineering business units. The flip-chart paper containing these outputs is tacked to the far right side of the wall.

Step 3: Define Inputs

The team then defines the major inputs that are used by the business to produce the outputs defined in Step 2. These inputs are recorded on flip-chart paper and tacked to the wall on the far left side. The team finds it best to look at each output one at a time and decide what inputs are needed to produce the output; this way they will not overlook any inputs. The inputs they identified in this case include labor, funding, client needs, and technologies. Client needs are the most typical input of all businesses. These needs are usually made known in engineering by direct sales calls and in RFPs (requests for proposal), which are written documents provided by prospective clients. Thus, the engineering business unit has to write a proposal outlining their response to specific client needs, such as a project to clean up a waste site.

Other inputs for this sample business include the labor market for staffing jobs the business unit will perform, funds needed to do the work, and technologies (e.g., a way to burn pollutants) that will be used to meet the client needs. Note to the right of each input (on an arrow) that the team has included a word or more that tells what the input is used for. For instance, the "Technologies" inputs provide new or existing ways to meet clients needs. In this example, new technologies are important as an input that keeps the business in line with, or ahead of, the competition (a condition). When the team has specified all the inputs, they are then ready to go to the next step.

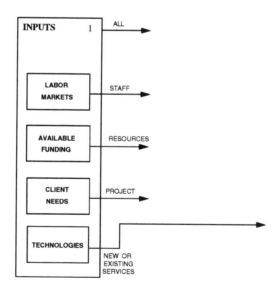

Step 4: Define Conditions

The team defines all the conditions that affect the use of the inputs they defined in Step 3. They also define the conditions that have an impact on the process, which is defined in a subsequent step. Conditions are defined under the label "Doing-Business Influences." Typical conditions include government regulations, which range from very specific requirements that affect some processes to more general requirements (e.g., health and safety regulations) affecting all of the business. This engineering business unit must observe numerous federal and state government environmental regulations, as well as any local codes. Also, it must take into consideration the public's concern for environmental issues, the economy in general, and competing corporations. These are all conditions to which the business must pay attention in executing process, and that affect how inputs are maintained and handled. The business cannot generally change conditions, but in some instances it may influence changes. For example, an environmental business may ask the government to change or append regulations for a specific project.

Once the team has defined all the conditions, it may go on to the next step. Of course, as the team works through the business-unit work diagram and gains new insights into the business, it may (and usually does) return to previous steps and modify what it has specified.

Before proceeding to Step 5, the team tacks the defined conditions to the wall just above the inputs list.

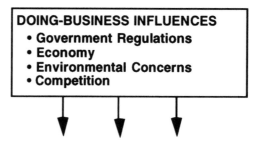

DOING-BUSINESS INFLUENCES
- **Government Regulations**
- **Economy**
- **Environmental Concerns**
- **Competition**

Step 5: Define Consequences

Once the team knows the outputs, inputs, and conditions, it needs to define the desired results that the business wants to achieve in the form of positive consequences.

Representative consequences for a business unit generally fall into two categories: (1) those that relate to client satisfaction, and (2) those that the business wants to achieve for itself (for its own satisfaction). Consequences are, or should be, a direct reflection of the mission of a business. The following are representative consequences for a business, most of which apply to the sample environmental engineering business.

Client Consequences

– Client satisfaction
– Return policy guarantee —"No questions asked."
– "Best price"
– Within budget

Business Consequences

– Profit
– X% of market share
– Employee satisfaction
– Growth

Of course, consequences can be more specific than those stated here. The team defines the consequences for the business unit, writes these on flip-chart paper, and tacks them to the wall to the right of the outputs.

Step 6: Define Process

Process links inputs and outputs and is affected by business conditions. The team defines process by taking one output at a time and, beginning with the inputs that produce the output, tracing what exists in the business to produce the output. Generally, this means defining what work groups exist to process the inputs to the outputs. For example, as illustrated below for the complete process of the sample business, in producing the engineering design output, the team defines the process as going through sales and marketing, proposal development, management, engineering, and the complete project management cycle (to be described shortly). The work diagram's process section, shown below, encompasses everything between inputs and outputs. It may look somewhat complicated at first, but a brief explanation will help you see that process is not at all that difficult to portray and understand.

Typically, process at the Business Unit level is composed of the flow and interaction between the major work groups that make up the business unit. Knowing what to put in the process would, at first glance, seem to be a matter of having a box for each major work group; however, there is some exception to this. Which work groups you include in this list and their level of detail is up to you. Although there is no specific guideline to tell you what the level of detail should be, it is worth noting that you are trying to visualize and communicate to yourself and others what your business is and does. Usually, analysis groups quickly come to an understanding of what level of detail makes sense and is therefore needed. Keep in mind that the very detailed analysis and definition of the business will come forth during subsequent analyses of the Work Group and Process levels—the subjects of Chapters 5 and 6, respectively.

In the sample process, we see major work groups for Human Resources, Proposal Development, Legal, Sales and Marketing, Engineering, and Business Unit Management. These are work groups with which most of us are familiar, as most business units have these kinds of work groups. But, there is a set of work groups that are organized in a special way. Special sets of work groups like this are referred to as "ways of doing business." They represent the processes of a business unit that are organized with work groups of related purpose to achieve specific process development. Here the "way of doing business" is designated as Project Management. It is "a way of doing business" employed by many major businesses, especially in engineering, construction, aerospace, and other businesses where a team approach is needed to accomplish major client projects. For example, project management is used by a construction business to erect a major building. The building is a "Project." You see the following representation of project management in the sample diagram:

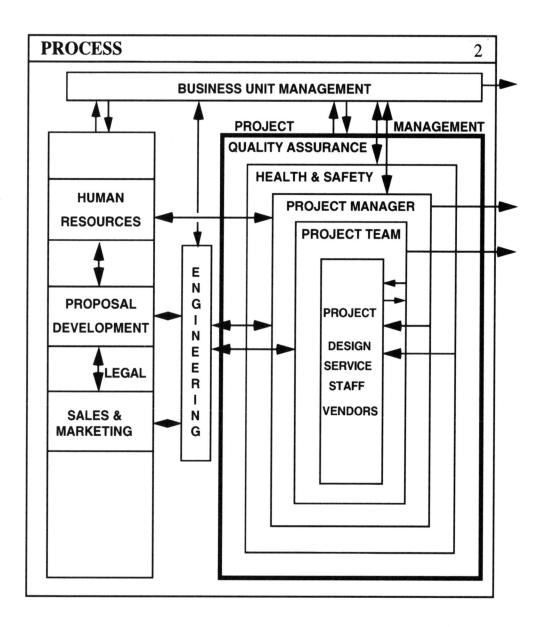

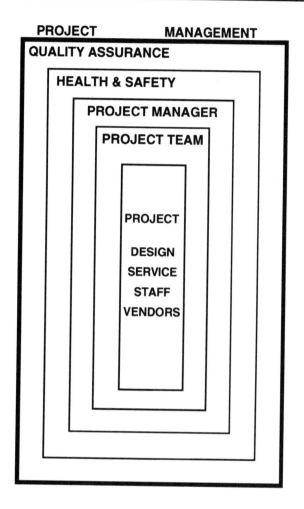

In the middle is the "Project" that will take the form of services and design. Then, Project is surrounded by a box for the Project Team, which in turn is surrounded by the Project Manager. These groups are governed by Health and Safety and Quality Assurance, which are represented by boxes surrounding the entire project. All of these groups work together in a project management role—a way of doing business. In the entire process definition, Project Management, as a team, interacts with other work groups such as Human Resources, Proposal Development, Engineering, and Management.

Finally, note in the display for the process in Figure 4.1 that arrows are used to link work groups and show which way process flows. For example, client needs (as an input) first come to Sales and Marketing, who then decide if Proposal Development will write a written proposal, cost proposal, or qualification description (or a combination thereof). Proposal Development works with Engineering, Legal, and Human Resources. The essential requirement is that for each output, there should be a logical flow from input(s) through process to achieve the output.

When the team has finished defining process, it places the process between inputs. It has almost finished its first draft definition of the business-unit work diagram.

Step 7: Define Feedback

The team now defines two major types of feedback for their business-unit work diagram. Feedback is usually indicated by these types of arrows:

First, one type of arrow is used to indicate where and when client satisfaction will be obtained after the output is delivered. The arrow in Section 6 (Feedback) of Figure 4.1 is used in this way. It extends from the bottom of the Outputs box into the Process box, moving in one direction. This indicates that the business seeks client information on their outputs to find out if clients are satisfied. This information is fed back to those in the work process. If positive feedback, it reinforces good use of process. If negative feedback, it tells the business either to correct something in its process (or other work elements) or to respond to the client in a way that will restore satisfaction, or to do both. Various means can be used to collect feedback, such as client satisfaction surveys, an 800 number, direct everyday contact, and mail-in feedback cards.

The second type of arrow indicates feedback within the process. It links work groups (the boxes in Section 2, Process) to indicate the flow of information—the feedback that is most often used within and between the work groups to improve processing and utilization of inputs. Such feedback arrows have two points, each moving in a different direction. For example, you see a double-pointed arrow between Proposal Development and Engineering. This means that when developing proposals, the proposal writer seeks information and feedback from Engineering on the accuracy of the technical data in the proposal writing effort. Or, it could mean that Engineering seeks information from the proposal development group to clarify a proposal that the project manager in Project Management is now using to execute as a project. Other feedback arrows link Proposal Development and Legal, Human Resources, and Project Management, and a number of other work groups. Several feedback loops connect Management (at the top of Process box) to other work groups within the process. The details of this feedback are specified either in descriptive form elsewhere or as part of other work diagrams for processes and work groups (which you will learn about in the next two chapters).

Step 8: Collect Comments

With this step, the Business Unit Analysis team completes the first draft of the business-unit work diagram. The team should now divide up the business in some logical way and assign a section to each member of the team. Members then take the first draft of the work diagram to others in the business and ask for their comments on all aspects of the work diagram. These comments are brought back to the analysis team and used to refine the first draft.

Step 9: Consensus

The analysis team continues to refine the first draft until everyone agrees that the work diagram represents an accurate definition of the business unit. Figure 4.1 is a representative sample of a business-unit work diagram that was produced with consensus by an analysis team. As described later in this chapter, the team will have other steps and tasks to perform in using the business-unit work diagram to institute quality improvements.

The Sequence for Developing a Business-Unit Work Diagram

The order in which a team defines the six elements of a work diagram is critical. The order for discussion and consensus is as follows:

First:	**Outputs** *You have to agree upon the targets first and foremost.* This is another of those instances in which you have to DEFINE AUSTRALIA FIRST. For the business unit, this means specifying the primary outputs as services or products for which the business exists.
Second:	**Inputs** *You have to know what you need to produce the outputs.* Typically, inputs include client needs and resources for producing the outputs.
Third:	**Conditions** *What factors over which you have no control will affect the inputs and processing to produce the outputs?* At the Business Unit level, conditions may be stated in general terms. These conditions will then be defined in greater detail at the Process and Work Group levels. For most businesses, among general conditions there are company policies, competition, economy, government regulations, and the like.

Fourth:	**Consequences**

What desirable results do you want from the outputs for the benefit of the clients, the business, and those who work for the business?

These are best defined when you know what outputs the business will produce, what inputs are present, and how both are affected by certain conditions. Typical consequences for the business unit include, first and foremost, client satisfaction and those results that the business wants to achieve for itself.

Fifth:	**Process**

What processes, including appropriate technologies, will be used to produce the outputs, given the inputs and conditions, and considering the desired consequences?

For the business unit, there is an overall process that is encompassed by the work groups it has designed and designated to achieve its primary outputs (or that it will design and designate). An order is specified for the process, and the direction is indicated by the lines and arrows that connect the work groups.

Sixth:	**Feedback**

How will you collect information from your external client to assure that you have met their needs and can respond to their complaints or follow up service needs? How will you do the same for internal clients (within and between work groups) to assure that they will work together to do their best for the external client in the long run and each other in the short run?

Now that we have constructed a work diagram for a typical business unit, we need to consider an important step in improving a business unit, one that is closely linked to a work diagram: the step of measurement. This step has been included primarily because it is a necessary part of the continuous improvement processes that are widely used in today's business world. Measuring business activities and processes in order to identify and solve quality improvement needs is a growing activity of successful businesses. This step is referred to as the definition and use of "performance questions."

DEFINING PROCESS PERFORMANCE QUESTIONS FOR THE BUSINESS UNIT PROCESS

Guessing where to make improvements in a business is far less useful and accurate than careful measurement. It is not all that uncommon in business to hear workers and managers say, "I think that if we just changed [such and such], things would be a lot better." This may well be the case, but a better approach is to determine where and when to use accurate measurement techniques. Doing measurement for the sake of measurement, a practice sometimes found in TQM processes, is as much a mistake as not doing measurement at all.

Before we can begin measurement, we have to know what questions to ask. Knowing what questions to ask may be more difficult than you think. The following exercise, which you can conduct in your own business, will adequately demonstrate the difficulty of defining the right performance questions.

1.   Select a group of 20 or more workers and managers, and divide them into groups of five to seven.

2.   Ask each group to devise a set of questions that they would use to measure any one of the major work groups in your business. For example, have each group write a set of questions that could be used to measure whether the workers believe Human Resources, Project Management, Proposal Development, or another work group in their company is performing at the quality level it should be.

3.   Review the results. Be prepared to find that the groups have come up with almost completely different sets of questions.

This exercise very clearly points out two things: (1) Most workers don't know specifically what to measure in someone else's work group, let alone their own, and (2) what they do measure is usually an aspect of performance that is bothering them or of special interest to them as an individual or group. The latter is useful information for other purposes, but not for measuring the overall work performance of a specific work group. A better way of learning what to measure, and how, is needed. Fortunately, the work language provides us with a solid basis for knowing what to measure. We must simply decide the best and most accurate way to state the questions, and then proceed to measure them.

Performance questions should be defined for all parts of a business-unit work diagram. This includes inputs, conditions, processes, outputs, consequences, and feedback. Performance questions represent those questions the business needs to ask in order to measure whether each part of the work diagram—the business—is doing its work in the most effective and efficient manner. Put another way, the questions are the quality measurement points for the business. This measurement should include what will be referred to here as "the whole boat." To measure the whole boat means to measure and improve the entire work diagram, not just an element here or there. When the questions are answered, and if quality is not being achieved to a satisfactory level, then we have information indicating where the business as a whole should be improved.

With the proper frame of reference, the defining of performance questions can be accomplished with relative ease. Generally, most people have little difficulty knowing what to ask about inputs, conditions, outputs, consequences, and feedback. Process tends to be more difficult. Most of the following material will focus on defining performance questions for process. A brief description of all six elements of the work language will help you define performance questions for the business unit.

Defining performance questions for inputs is mainly a matter of measuring for their availability and development. For example, these are typical performance questions for client needs: "Does a systematic plan for identifying client needs for marketing purposes exist and produce satisfactory results?" "Are client needs clearly defined before projects commence?" "Are client needs being developed for future work as the project is being executed?" These questions address what is available as well as what needs to be developed in the business. Without these questions and the actual measurement of them, the business may (and often does) overlook needs and opportunities to improve and maintain itself.

Defining performance questions for outputs is mainly a matter of measuring completeness, accuracy, timeliness, and cost. Questions on output are designed to address the overall issue of quality for the business, work group, processes, or individuals. For example: "Did the report address the specific needs and requirements specified in the contract?" "Is the data accurate?" "Was the output delivered on time?" "Was the output produced within budget?"

Performance questions for conditions have unique requirements. Unlike the other work elements, conditions are usually preset for the business operations and cannot be changed. Consequently, we probably do not need to measure whether conditions exist, although in the case of company policies, some conditions might be missing. Most of the time the business first has to measure the individual awareness of the conditions, and then whether the conditions are being attended to during use of inputs and processing. The business does have control over worker and manager "awareness" of the conditions (provided workers and managers cooperate) and over assuring that the conditions are met. It is surprising how many businesses are not fully aware of conditions, which is one reason they get into so much trouble. For instance, environmental engineering businesses may get into trouble by not paying enough attention to government regulations, public concerns, safety, their competition, and where the economy is headed. The same may be said of many businesses where individuals do not pay attention to company policies.

A sample performance question for a condition would be, "Are we collecting data on where our competition is winning its business?" This is a condition that relates to the "client needs" input. What performance questions do you suppose should be asked to measure the effect of government regulations on the process used by the engineering company in Figure 4.1? There are many. For example, for the Business Unit Management work group, we could ask, "Is the business meeting EEO guidelines while doing its projects?"

As indicated above, there is a second step in defining and measuring questions related to conditions. It is one thing to be aware of the conditions; another to ensure they are being followed. Workers have to apply conditions to inputs and process in order to produce the outputs. Thus, a typical performance question for a condition related to inputs would be, "Do the inputs measure up to the standards applied by federal regulations?" Regarding the process, one question might be, "Are managers following EEO guidelines in hiring practices?"

Performance questions for consequences should center on relating the alignment of the other five elements of a work diagram to achieve satisfactory consequences. By *alignment* we mean how well inputs, conditions, process, outputs, and feedback collectively contribute to positive consequences, and how failure leads to negative consequences. Discerning the needed changes to improve consequences is often very difficult since the control of inputs, conditions, process, outputs, and feedback are so intertwined. Nonetheless, questions to measure consequences must be asked. For example, Ford Motor asked many questions about its intended consequences of the slogan "Quality Is Job One." These questions were probably similar to the following: "Does our output look and act like our standards of Job One?" "Are we following up with our current buyers to maintain our Job One reputation?" Businesses that fail to measure their consequences end up ignoring their clients—just ask Sears and several other major companies that have experienced business reversals and are in the process of trying to recover! Eventually, lack of client interest in a product or service will demand the business' attention (and measurement). Proactive businesses measure performance rather than wait for negative or positive consequences.

Performance questions for feedback center on whether questions are being asked, reinforcement given, and information shared, and if so, when they occur and in what forms. Businesses that merely pass their outputs from one work group to another, or that do not follow up with external clients, are the ones not asking and measuring performance questions about feedback. A typical feedback question is, "How efficient is our response mechanism to customer complaints?" Or even simpler, "How difficult is it for our clients to call us on the telephone?" A very important feedback question is, "Are our managers actively asking workers what kind of help they need with inputs and during processing, and when, where, and how they need this help?"

The above are general guidelines on performance questions for inputs, conditions, outputs, consequences, and feedback. As was suggested earlier, performance questions for process are a little harder to define for the average manager and worker. However, there is a simple "trick of the trade" employed by performance technologists that will make this task a lot simpler for you once you learn it.

Defining Process Performance Questions for the Business Unit Process

The Process section of a business-unit work diagram is composed of a set of work groups. Figure 4.1 includes work groups such as Human Resources, Proposal Development, Sales and Marketing, Engineering, Project Management (with its several layers), Legal, and Business Unit Management. As the performance question exercise illustrated, if we ask groups of managers and workers each to formulate a set of questions for work groups, we will receive dissimilar sets of questions. To avoid this, we need to first define the outputs of the various work groups. Let us take one of the work groups from Figure 4.1 and see what is meant by work group outputs, and what performance questions we would formulate to measure these outputs.

In Figure 4.2 there is a list of the outputs and their corresponding performance questions written from the outputs. These questions would be used to measure the Human Resources, Proposal Development, and Sales and Marketing work groups in Figure 4.1. For the purpose of illustration, we will look at the outputs and corresponding performance question for the Human Resources work group, since this is a work group with which most of us are familiar. Monica, our sample worker, is a part of Human Resources.

The first question in Figure 4.2 is, "Are in-house resumes available/updated?" This is a performance question related to the Human Resources output of "resumes." This question is important in a project management-oriented business such as an engineering company. Why? Resumes are important both for proposal writing and finding the right people to work on approved projects. Thus, the Human Resources work group is responsible for, and partially measured in its overall success by, meeting the requirements of this question. Should the answer to this question demonstrate that Human Resources is not providing timely or complete resumes, a needed change (improvement) would be suggested.

The idea behind formulating the proper question is simply one of first determining the output, then determining how the output is utilized—usually, what the internal or external client does with the given output. In the example of Human Resources, the client is an internal one (such as a project manager) that uses the output (resumes) as his or her input (qualified candidates) to do the work (to fill project positions, leading eventually to the execution of the project). The pertinent question therefore is, "Are in-house resumes available/updated?" Let us look at another example and have you determine the performance question.

PERFORMANCE QUESTIONS FOR WORK GROUPS

Outputs	Performance Questions
	Human Resources
• Resumes	1. Are in-house resumes available/updated?
• Performance review plans	2. Are workers provided meaningful performance reviews annually?
	3. Are the workers receiving needed training and other performance improvement programs to establish or maintain skills and to obtain the knowledge to perform future job needs?
• Training program/ Performance improvement programs	
• Career development plans	4. Given growth plans, are workers provided career development opportunities?
• Compensation package	5. Are compensation expectations clearly defined?
• Salary ranges	6. Are salary ranges fair to competition standards?
• Flexplan	7. Is the "flexplan" meeting work needs for health care relative to business ability to provide?
• Recruiting Program	8. Are we able to recruit skilled employees to meet general business and project contract requirements?
• Employees Hired	9. Are skilled employees hired?
	Proposal Development
• Proposals	1. Are winning proposals developed?
• Proposal reviews	2. Are proposals legally correct?
• Oral presentations	3. Are individuals and teams prepared to give winning oral presentations?
• Visuals for proposals	4. Are visuals prepared that enhance proposal communication and oral presentation?
	Sales and Marketing
	1. Is a marketing plan prepared and reviewed annually?
	2. Does Marketing conduct market research?
• Marketing plans	3. Is the competition evaluated on a regular basis?
• Market research	4. Are new market opportunities evaluated semi-annually?
• Competition reviews	5. Do marketing opportunities match staffing/planning?
• New Market studies	6. Is office staff given orientations to marketing plans?
• Manpower studies	7. Once market areas are identified, are resources made available to develop them?
• Marketing orientations	— Operations support personnel and equipment
• Resources plans	— Salespeople
	— Brochures, etc.

Figure 4.2

You will recall that one of Lee's outputs as a proposal writer in the Proposal Development work group is to produce cost proposals (see Chapter 3, Figure 3.1 or 3.5). What question should be asked to measure this output? Think in terms of the critical question of what cost proposals represent to the business unit. How will a client of Lee's use the cost proposal? Keep in mind, at this time we are considering the business unit, not the individual. Which of the following would be the best performance question about cost proposals?

- Does the cost proposal have all the critical components to make it a good cost proposal?

- Are our cost proposals competitive with others to win new projects and realize a reasonable profit?

- Does proposal development seek the input of all the necessary parties in the business unit to develop good cost proposals?

All of these are good questions about cost proposals; however, when measuring output you need to consider what purpose the output serves for the business unit (or individual or work group). In this case, the second question is the best performance question. If our cost proposals are not competitive with others, then the business unit can neither win new projects nor profitably carry out new projects. Remember: When formulating performance questions, first define the output for a work group; then, frame the question in terms of how that output is used by the client of the work group.

The Sequence for Defining Performance Questions

The method through which the performance questions are determined can, in itself, help improve the business. This method employs a specific order for formulating the questions. The following is a description of how this method is used and what this order can contribute.

1. After the Business Unit Analysis team has been oriented to the nature and scope of performance questions—a step that is vital to do right—team members are asked to define, initially alone and then with others outside the team, the performance questions for their *own work group*. They write questions related only to their own outputs, thereby providing a profile of what the individual work group sees as its specific responsibilities (accountabilities) *and how they are measured*. In point of fact, while this has been described as if individuals were defining questions in isolation, in reality they are holding discussions outside their team meetings with others within their work groups. This provides greater accuracy in defining the right questions and, at the same time, helps gain "buy-in" to what is being defined and will be measured for the entire business unit.

2. Once the performance questions for their own work group have been defined, they are directed to define performance questions about other work groups that serve as an *input* to their own. Again, these questions are formulated and contents defined by knowing the outputs of a work group that provides the inputs.

3. Next, each team member's group develops performance questions for work groups to which they are an *output*.

4. Finally, they are asked to write "general performance questions" that may cut across and between various work groups.

Note again the order in this suggested approach. First, the performance questions for your own work group are formulated. Then, the questions for work groups that supply you with an input. Next, questions for work groups to which you supply an output. Finally, performance questions that cut across various groups are formulated.

Having defined these performance questions individually, the Business Unit Analysis team collaborates to discuss each work group one by one and to formulate a set of final questions upon which they can all agree. This order of defining and discussing questions serves many purposes, including (1) clarification of one's own responsibilities and the perception of the responsibilities of others; (2) establishment of ownership for what one is responsible for and will be measured by; (3) development of quality measurements; (4) the addition, subtraction, or realignment of responsibilities; and (5), in some instances, the solution to some individual and group work problems.

One of the more interesting aspects of this method is that it is a "safe" way for those in the business to express how they would improve work—their own and that of others—without appearing to be critical; the suggestions come in the form of questions. This method also encourages the more shy people with good ideas to speak up. Nearly everyone in a business has ideas about how they think others could be doing work better. When couched in the form of performance questions, these opinions come out in the form of proposed measurements rather than criticism. More important, however, is the clarity of roles and ownership that is established.

It cannot be emphasized enough that the formulation of performance questions requires an exacting and careful process. To simply turn everyone loose to define any and all questions they want to would be a mistake. Should you go that route, you will end up measuring areas that simply do not need to be measured and only subparts of important activities that should be measured. Thus, it is far better to define outputs first, then formulate questions to the outputs in terms of their use.

THE "WHOLE BOAT MUST RISE" CONCEPT

Before this chapter on Business Unit Analysis comes to a close, there is an important concept concerning the value of defining and measuring a business unit that should be described: the "Whole Boat Must Rise" concept. As a basis for understanding this concept, think of how frustrating it is when one part of the business lags behind the other in quality—for instance, when at the macro level of a business, the service department cannot keep up with customer complaints or the sales force cannot sell an otherwise excellent product. This frustration can also occur at the micro level, when the manager is a good guy but can't plan his way out of a wet paper bag.

Are these individual problems or problems that affect the whole business? The answer is the latter—the whole of the business suffers. It is not good business practice to improve the quality of work in one area (e.g., process or work group), only to see it subsequently messed up in another area. It is best to improve quality at *all* levels. And what about those things that take an inordinate amount of time and effort to fix? Should we be content in business to go around fighting small fires all the time? The answer is no!

What the Language of Work provides us is a way out of this seemingly never-ending process of fixing here and there. This is accomplished by analyzing the whole of the business (the business unit), and then each of the other levels (work groups, processes, and individuals) of the Business Sphere. We are able to measure and improve the whole business on a continuing basis because, through our four-level application of work diagrams, we know what constitutes the business and how to measure it by means of performance questions. This is the Whole Boat Must Rise approach to business improvement. The point is, if you want to improve a business, you have to identify and work on all the quality improvement needs and, thus, make all of the business rise within and between all four levels—the Whole Boat Must Rise approach in its broadest and most complete sense. This is best accomplished by understanding, measuring, and strengthening the business through the Language of Work.

BENEFITS OF USING THE LANGUAGE OF WORK ON THE BUSINESS UNIT LEVEL

Using a common work language in the form of work diagrams and performance questions to improve a business unit is a systematic approach to improving the effectiveness and efficiency of the entire business unit. As the forerunner to an analysis of work groups, processes, and individuals, Business Unit Analysis helps us assure that the business is headed in the right direction of meeting internal and external client satisfaction before setting out to improve other levels of the Business Sphere.

For management and workers, analyzing a business unit can do the following:

- Clarify expectations and responsibilities related to overall business inputs, conditions, processes, outputs, consequences, and feedback

- Build the kind of mutual respect and trust so necessary for establishing a truly committed work force

- Provide a clear understanding of how workers and managers will be measured relative to inputs, conditions, processes, outputs, consequences, and feedback

- Provide the means to measure against output to and from internal and external clients

For the business as a whole, analyzing the business unit through the use of the work-diagram application tool provides far and away the most systematic approach to identifying and interrelating needed improvements. Large lists of quality improvement needs can be derived from brainstorming or simply asking workers and managers to make suggestions. These are useful techniques because employees feel like they are making a contribution. But only a systematic process such as work diagramming can help assure that all aspects of the business are looked at for improvement. Only a systematic analysis can help show us the work group and individual *relationships* within the business and where these relationships must be improved. And because one solution in one work group of a business does affect another work group, knowing the relationships is important. Remember: Business performance is made up of one group's output affecting another group's input and subsequent output; therefore, a quality solution in one group does affect another. The independent, one-department approach to solving problems is simply inadequate if the business is to improve as a whole—the Whole Boat Must Rise concept. Looking at, and making improvements on, the Business Unit level assures an "interdependent" view of work groups that make up a business. The goal of a business is, after all, to operate as a unit, not a bunch of cells. In the next chapter, "Applying the Language of Work to Work Groups," we will see how the work group "cells" can be interrelated and improved.

CHAPTER 5

APPLYING THE LANGUAGE OF WORK TO WORK GROUPS

In this chapter we will look closely at how to apply the Language of Work to work groups. Work groups, as an integral part of the Business Sphere, are those divisions of labor and other resources that the business uses to organize itself to accomplish its processes and manage the work force. Work groups usually match the business' organization chart. However, there are some kinds of work groups not found on a typical organization chart, such as combinations of work groups that make up a project management team, cross-functional work groups, or other team approaches to work.

All businesses need to be analyzed at the right level of detail if they are to define, measure, and improve themselves. For the Business Unit Analysis, we specified the right level of analysis as:

- The overall outputs of the business

- The necessary major inputs to produce the outputs

- The governing conditions that prevail and influence inputs and and process

- The overall consequences the business desires to achieve

- The basic work groups that make up the process

- The necessary feedback to check on client satisfaction and to refine process execution

The Business Unit level was primarily concerned with overall business goals and their attainment. In this chapter, Work Group Analysis will provide the next level of detail: measuring and making improvements to the *organizational structure* of the business. In defining and examining work groups at the Business Unit level, such as Human Resources, Proposal Development, and Sales and Marketing, we determined the outputs and looked at how to use Business Unit Analysis to measure the performance of these work groups. However, each of these work groups, in and of itself, involves many more things that need definition and measurement, such as their own inputs, conditions, process, consequences, and feedback. Work Group Analysis is where we define this further level of detail needed to improve the work groups. Some examples of work-group work diagrams will help you see when, where, and why this level of detail is needed. But, before moving on to this, two other benefits of Work Group Analysis should be mentioned.

Work Group Analysis shows us where to measure the *relationships* within and between work groups, which the broader analysis at the Business Unit level cannot show us. As most businesses experience work-group relationship problems, you are probably familiar with scenarios similar to the following: the print shop that is given work by various work groups who complain, "The print shop never gets my work out on time!" Or the engineering group that "doesn't get the drawing to the project staff in a final form without all those darn changes!" Or the accounting department that "can't process a simple purchase order payment on time or with the data that my client needs!" Since these relationships between work groups are so often critical to the success of a business, knowing clearly the relationships and measuring them will show us where to improve business in a significant way.

Another benefit of Work Group Analysis is that it helps workers and managers achieve a clearer understanding of the Work Group level—the level at which managers typically plan and administer, and at which workers are organized to do work. If just a Business Unit Analysis were done, executives would benefit (for they operate at the Business Unit level most of the time) and workers and managers would gain some insight into the overall strategy and mission of the business, but the business would suffer from a serious oversight: not providing workers and managers with information essential to their understanding of *the level at which they operate* in the business. Work Group Analysis supplies this information. It makes the difference between simply telling workers, "Here's the mission; now follow it," and informing them of the mission and *how* the mission will be achieved—which they clearly need to know.

As a final introductory comment to Work Group Analysis, it is strongly recommended that you do a Business Unit, a Process, and an Individual Analysis before doing a Work Group Analysis. Business Unit Analysis, of course, must be done first so that the overall mission of the business is known—DEFINE AUSTRALIA FIRST! Then, the processes are defined so that we know how to achieve the major outputs. Next, individuals are defined to carry out the processes. Only after these have been done can you then know how to best organize the work groups to achieve efficiency and effectiveness of the processes used by individuals to achieve overall business-unit outputs.

To understand how a typical analysis on the Work Group level is conducted, we will focus on the Human Resources work group from the engineering business unit diagrammed in Figure 4.1—the work group to which Monica, the trainer, belongs. The following discussion will cover defining the six work elements in a work diagram and then measuring these elements using performance questions (the basic method used in Business Unit Analysis). This will help us learn what *level of detail* we need for Work Group Analysis and what kind of *work group relationships* we should focus on.

WORK GROUP ANALYSIS—USING THE WORK DIAGRAM APPROACH

Let us first review the different work groups from the process section of the sample business unit work diagram in Figure 4.1 (see page 101). The work groups include Human Resources, Proposal Development, Sales and Marketing, Management, Legal, Engineering, and Project Management (which included the work groups of Quality Assurance, Health and Safety, Project Manager, and the Project Team). All work groups, no matter what their size, need Work Group Analysis, for we must determine the specific inputs, process, conditions, consequences, and feedback that result in or from the outputs that were defined during Business Unit Analysis.

Figure 5.1, on the following page, is a detailed version of a work diagram for the Human Resources work group. It represents, for illustrative purposes, a detailed breakdown of the work group into Employment, Training, Benefits, and Compensation (of course, in your business, HR may be divided differently and have fewer or more parts to it). We will now look at how this sample work-group work diagram was created.

Outputs

In Figure 4.2, "Performance Questions for Work Groups," nine outputs were listed for Human Resources (see page 115). We see in Figure 5.1 that the management of the sample engineering business has categorized the nine outputs under four smaller work groups: Employment, Training, Benefits, and Compensation. Their outputs are shown in the following table.

Work Group	Outputs
Employment	Resumes
	Performance Reviews
	Recruitment Program
	Employees Hired
Training	Training Programs/Performance
	Improvement Programs (PIP)
	Career Development Plans

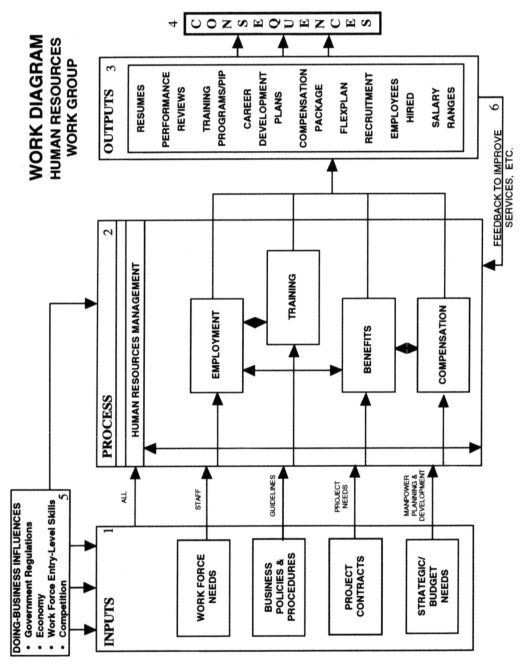

Figure 5.1

| Compensation | Compensation Package |
| | Salary Ranges |

| Benefits | Flexplan (a kind of benefit enrollment system) |

From this example, we can begin to see that during Business Unit Analysis we define the "big picture" of work groups as they constitute the primary *process* of the business unit. During Work Group Analysis we define the *details,* including the six work elements, of each individual work group.

It is crucial that the details of the Work Group Analysis are based on the general outputs of the Business Unit Analysis. These general outputs form the basis on which other specific work groups are formed. For example, Human Resources was formed to help achieve various business outputs related to Project Management and the overall operations of other work groups. Then, in the Work Group Analysis, Human Resources was further divided into the work groups of Employment, Training, Compensation, and Benefits, with the outputs in Figure 5.1 based on the outputs in Figure 4.2. This division would increase in detail as we move from Business Unit to Work Group Analysis, and can best be understood as our way of tracing the "cascading" of work, particularly outputs, down into the business. Thus the details we focus on in Work Group Analysis can be defined as specific outputs that originate from the general outputs of the business unit.

This cascading down into business at successive levels of detail using a common work-language approach is one of the powerful advantages of having a work language. In this way, workers and managers begin to understand outputs at all levels and how one output affects another output as its input. Cascading also helps managers and workers understand why an orientation to internal client satisfaction to achieve quality is so important. Each person's output is a critical input to one or more internal clients, and each client should be given the best output that can be delivered; otherwise, there will be quality problems as work cascades through the business. Once workers and managers see how various outputs relate, they begin to see that the same holds true for the rest of the Business Sphere, including specific inputs, conditions, process, consequences, and feedback. Everything in business has a way of affecting everything else in a manner that needs to be understood and acted upon. And, to truly improve a business, these relationships must be identified, enhanced, and reinforced.

Thus far we know that we should begin Work Group Analysis by referring to the outputs of the business determined during Business Unit Analysis, in the definition of the performance questions. These outputs appear on the right side of the work-group work diagram. Those for Human Resources in Figure 5.1 follow on the next page.

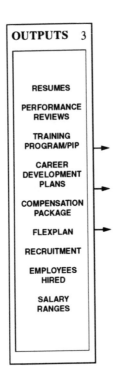

Having placed the outputs in this location on the work diagram, the analysis team would then define in order (which is crucial) the inputs, conditions, consequences, process, and feedback that are needed to achieve the outputs. Let us see what was defined by a team through a Work Group Analysis for the other five elements of work in the Human Resources work group.

Inputs

To produce the outputs, certain inputs are needed, and these are listed on the left side of the work diagram. As shown here, the inputs include Work Force Needs, Business Policies and Procedures, Project Contracts, and Strategic/Budget Needs. Why these particular inputs?

Work groups typically derive their primary inputs from client needs, as do business units. In the case of Human Resources, work force needs are grouped as one primary input. These may stem directly from the personal needs of workers, but usually are determined by the facilitation needs of managers. For instance, a manager may determine that specific numbers and kinds of workers will need training to execute processes better. Although these needs generally originate with managers, in today's businesses the increased emphasis on work teams may shift the primary source of these needs to the work team. Work force needs will affect every function of the Human Resources process.

126

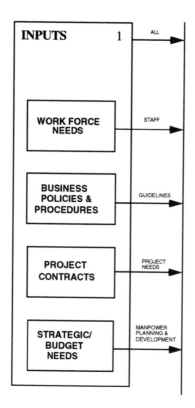

Listing business policies and procedures under inputs may seem odd, as usually these are categorized as conditions. Their inclusion here merely indicates that Human Resources is, or can be, a direct "arm" of administration for *implementing* policies and procedures and ensuring certain business conditions are met. In general, whenever a work group is responsible for implementing conditions, those conditions will become an input for the work group. Also, the work group may have some control over changing a policy or procedure, although the administration has the final authority. For example, for the function of hiring, there must be someone in the business who assures that Equal Employment Opportunity practices are known and followed. While this is a specific "condition" to be followed by all managers, the Human Resources work group must view EEO needs as an input to meet one of their primary outputs: assuring the employment of a properly constituted work force.

Another input typical of many work groups is their need to respond to internal projects or the needs of other work groups. In the engineering business, the project needs require the Human Resources work group to fill work force and training needs. Outputs such as resumes and competitive compensation will be particularly useful in meeting this kind of an input.

Conditions

The conditions are fairly typical. They include the following:

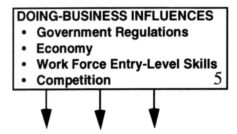

In this particular example, work force entry-level skills were listed since these conditions affect a number of inputs and processes used to achieve the outputs. For example, lower entry-level skills determine what level of training will be required. It may also affect the rate of compensation, the benefits that will be provided, and the degree of difficulty in employing the right kinds of workers and managers needed by the business.

Consequences

Consequences for Human Resources are not shown on the work diagram in Figure 5.1, but are fairly typical in nature. Among other possibilities, these might include:

- Employee satisfaction with performance reviews and meeting career development desires and needs

- A motivated work force

- Benefits that meet business, personal, and family needs

- Project Manager satisfaction in meeting contract needs for manpower, training, benefits, and compensation

Process

The Process section, which links outputs and inputs, is composed of the groups that make up the Human Resources work group. These include Employment, Training, Benefits, and Compensation. Of course, businesses choose to define, organize, and arrange this process differently, and the work groups shown here are only a representative example.

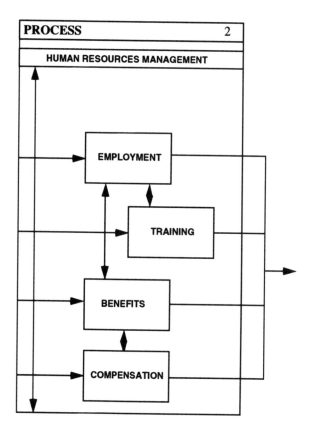

Feedback

As in the business-unit work diagram (Figure 4.1), there are two kinds of feedback. One kind of feedback extends from outputs (and consequences) to process:

FEEDBACK TO IMPROVE 6
SERVICES, ETC.

This represents the feedback from internal or external clients that tells you if your outputs are being received at an acceptable level of satisfaction and whether an improvement in service or product is needed.

The other kind of feedback is indicated by the use of double-pointed arrows in the Process section, as shown below.

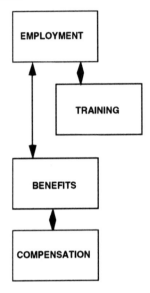

These are "loops" that connect such areas as Employment and Training, Employment and Benefits, and Benefits and Compensation. These feedback loops will be explored further in the upcoming explanation of measurement and work group relationships.

Once the analysis team has completed the first draft of the work diagram for Human Resources, they should share the draft with everyone in this work group, with representatives of internal clients, and with those who make inputs into Human Resources. They will be looking for clarification and agreement. When finalized, they proceed to the next step: deciding how to measure the work group for quality improvement.

DEFINITION OF PERFORMANCE QUESTIONS FOR WORK GROUPS

Measuring work group performance involves exactly the same technique and order previously described in defining performance questions for the business unit; therefore, only a few of the guiding principles will be stressed again here. Important details particular to defining performance measures for work groups, such as how to measure work group relationships, will also be included.

Note first of all that in Figure 5.1 the outputs were measured during the Business Unit Analysis (the questions used to do the measurement were specified in Figure 4.2). The results of that measurement tell us which outputs are not up to standards and need particular attention. The following example will help illustrate this and the application of measurement toward making quality improvements at the Work Group level.

Suppose results from Business Unit Analysis indicate that the first output of Human Resources, Resumes, is not up to performance standards. To answer the performance question "Are in-house resumes available/updated?" our analysis team actually went out and talked to various users of the resumes (project managers, managers hiring or assigning workers to tasks, and so forth). They found that only in 60 percent of the cases where resumes were needed to fill a new job position or to put in a proposal were there up-to-date resumes available. This measurement indicates that the Resume output is not being satisfactorily met as a business need and responsibility of the Employment work group. The Work Group Analysis team must therefore find out why and correct the problem.

The Work Group Analysis team must now measure the other work elements of the work-group work diagram—inputs, conditions, process, consequences, and feedback. As stated previously, we employ the measurement techniques described in Chapter 4. Special considerations for the measurement of work groups are detailed below. We will look at process first.

Process includes the four groups that make up the Human Resources work group: Employment, Training, Benefits, and Compensation. To measure process, we must first define the specific outputs for each group. Figure 5.2, on the following page lists a typical set of outputs for our sample business—your business would, of course, define some of these differently. For example, the Training group, of which Monica, the trainer, is a part, produces outputs that include:

- Training programs

- Employee orientation

- Work group measurements

- Performance improvement programs

Let us compare these outputs to Monica's outputs to illustrate how the outputs at all levels of a business relate to one another. If we consult Monica's work diagram (Figure 3.3, page 63), we see this individual is responsible for the following outputs:

OUTPUTS FOR THE
HUMAN RESOURCES WORK GROUP

OUTPUTS

Employment

1. Employee hiring
2. Recruitment programs
3. Resumes

Training

1. Training programs
2. Employee orientation
3. Work group measurements
4. Performance improvement programs

Benefits

1. Employee enrollment
2. Benefits program administration
3. Conflict resolutions
4. Cost-savings strategies

Compensation

1. Wage surveys
2. Wage adjustments
3. Grade levels assigned
4. Job descriptions
5. Wage discrepancies settled
6. Employees paid

Figure 5.2

- Stand-up training

- Written materials

- AV aids

- Job aids

- Measurement results

Observe that Monica's outputs all relate to the Training group outputs. For example, in developing training programs for her work group, she produces written materials, AV aids, and job aids, and conducts stand-up training. Also note that she uses some of these same outputs to produce other Training group outputs, such as employee orientation programs and performance improvement programs. Seeking out the relationship of outputs at all levels of a business is important not only to identify effective and efficient flow through the organization to the ultimate customer, but also to make sure we are measuring and improving the work groups, processes, and individuals who are in the business. In this case, we have seen that the general output at the Business Unit level of Products and Services relates in some part to the specific outputs of the Human Resources work group, which in turn relate to the Training work group, and finally to the individual position of a trainer. It is best to begin tracing output at the Business Unit level and cascade our way through the Process, Individual, and Work Group levels. One of the powers of the Language of Work is that it enables us to do this tracing and measurement of work elements accurately and meaningfully.

Once we have defined the outputs for each work group in the Process section of the work-group work diagram, we can define the performance questions for each output. Figure 5.3, on the next page, provides a list of performance questions for each of the four work groups from Figure 5.2. For example, in the Training work group, the first output, Training Programs, is to be measured by the corresponding question "Are skills training programs available to meet employee needs as shown in performance reviews and career development plans?" Note that the performance question is specified in such a manner that it reflects how the output is used by the client who receives it. In this example, the clients (employees) need the skills training (as input) in response to the outputs of a performance review or for their overall job development and as part of their career development plan. You can see from this example that the Language of Work again demonstrates the relationship between various inputs and outputs in the business, even at the micro level.

PERFORMANCE QUESTIONS FOR
WORK GROUP OUTPUTS

PERFORMANCE QUESTIONS

Employment
1. Are skilled employees hired?
2. Are recruitment programs successful and cost effective?
3. Are in-house resumes available/updated?

Training
1. Are skills training programs available to enhance employee needs as shown in performance reviews and career development plans?
2. Are new employee orientations provided?
3. Are evaluations conducted for work elements?
4. Are effective performance improvement programs developed and implemented for business work- element needs?

Benefits
1. Are employees enrolled in company programs?
2. Are benefits programs administered to work force satisfaction?
3. Are conflicts resolved?
4. Are cost-savings strategies proposed?

Compensation
1. Are wage surveys conducted?
2. Are wage adjustment proposals formulated?
3. Are jobs graded?
4. Are job descriptions written and kept up to date?
5. Are wage discrepancies resolved?
6. Are employees paid on time?

Figure 5.3

As for defining the performance questions for inputs, conditions, outputs, consequences, and feedback, you may follow the guidelines already described in Chapter 4. Before closing this chapter, there is one benefit of Work Group Analysis that needs special emphasis: improving work relationships within and between various work groups.

IMPROVING RELATIONSHIPS WITHIN AND BETWEEN WORK GROUPS

Work group relationships are formed *between* work groups when they share processes and when they hand off outputs to one another. Relationships also occur *within* a work group. Our sample business-unit work diagram (Figure 4.1) depicts relationships between work groups such as Human Resources and Proposal Development, Proposal Development and Sales and Marketing, and Proposal Development and Engineering.

The work-group work diagram in Figure 5.1 depicts the relationships between Employment and Training, Employment and Benefits, and Benefits and Compensation. It is important to define, measure, and improve these relationships because they create many of the problems that eventually lead to poor output performance. While work diagrams for the business unit and work groups are important for *showing* where relationships exist, there is a more succinct way to define and measure these relationships: the work relationship map.

A typical work relationship map is shown in Figure 5.4. It is built around the list of performance questions that are used to measure the work groups that are part of Human Resources. Determining the relationships is rather simple. If we look at the performance questions in Figure 5.4, we see that the Work Group Analysis team has linked the performance questions that clearly have a relationship; these are shown by lines that connect the questions. The team could have used outputs to link the relationship, but using performance questions to do this provides added and necessary detail to make linking that much easier and to assure greater accuracy. There are two types of relationships shown here, plus a reference to other work group relationships—in this example, work groups external to Human Resources. We will look at the two primary types of relationships first.

1. The first type of relationship is called "Interwork Group Relationships." Lines are used to link these relationships. For example, the first performance question in Employment is linked to the four outputs in Training. Note that at the bottom of the map, a performance question has been defined to measure the relationship between "skilled employees being hired" as a part of Employment and "skills training programs" as a part of Training. This question is identified as the link between performance question E1 (Employment question 1) and T1 (Training question 1). The question measures the relationship that should exist between the two specific outputs shared by Employment and Training.

2. The second type of relationship occurs within work groups and is called "Intrawork Group Relationships." Lines are also used to link these relationships. For example, within Compensation you see a relationship between

135

RELATIONSHIPS WITHIN AND BETWEEN WORK GROUPS
(INCLUDING SAMPLE PERFORMANCE QUESTIONS)

INTRAWORK/INTERWORK GROUP RELATIONSHIPS	LINKAGE GROUP RELATIONSHIPS

Employment (E)

1. Are skilled employees hired? — Proj. Mgmt.
2. Are recruitment programs successful and cost effective?
3. Are in-house resumes available/updated?

Training (T)

1. Are skills training programs available to enhance employee needs as shown in performance reviews and career development plans? — All Managers
2. Are new employee orientations provided? — Mgmt.
3. Are evaluations conducted for work elements?
4. Are effective performance improvement programs developed and implemented for business work-element needs? — Mgmt.

Benefits (B)

1. Are employees enrolled in company programs? — Payroll
2. Are benefits programs administered to work force satisfaction? — TQM Adm.
3. Are conflicts resolved? — Legal
4. Are cost-savings strategies proposed? — Exec. Mgmt.

Compensation (C)

1. Are wage surveys conducted? — Exec. Mgmt.
2. Are wage adjustment proposals formulated?
3. Are jobs graded?
4. Are employees given performance reviews and career development plans? — Mgmt.
5. Are job descriptions written and kept up to date? — Proj. Mgmt.
6. Are wage discrepancies resolved?
7. Are employees paid appropriate to the market? — Exec. Mgmt.

Examples of Typical Relationship Questions

Intrawork Group

E1-T1 What skill deficiencies need to be filled between entry-level skills and on-the-job training?

Interwork Group

C1-C2 Are wage adjustments formulated against timely wage surveys?

Figure 5.4

output one and two. Wage surveys are related to wage adjustments. A performance question for this relationship is shown at the bottom of the map, designated by "C1-C2" (Compensation 1 and 2).

The map lists and shows the relationships within and between four work groups of Human Resources; however, Human Resources, along with its four work groups, has relationships with work groups other than its own. For instance, it has working relationships with Project Management, Legal, and so forth. The size of the paper we must use prevents us from showing these relationships. We can, however, as shown on the right side of the map, reference various work groups. I call these relationships between major work groups Linkage Group Relationships. For example, output number one of Employment would have a relationship with Project Management that needs to be shown and measured. This relationship would need to be specified on another work relationship map (which can be number-coordinated for ease of reference). As appropriate, next to each work group output for Human Resources are listed other work groups to which each output would flow and become an input. As a point of reference, the Linkage Group relationships are those indicated in the flow diagrams by the arrows that are used to link work groups. Relationships will also show up later in the following chapter on Process Analysis, again demonstrating how the use of the Language of Work, through various application tools at different business levels, allows the business to "link" and measure activities and people where it makes sense. Making this linkage visible is a more powerful tool for identifying, measuring, and improving the business than could ever be achieved by examining only an organization chart, individual processes, or isolated work groups.

BENEFITS OF USING THE LANGUAGE OF WORK ON THE WORK GROUP LEVEL

Workers and managers can expect these benefits (and more) from Work Group Analysis:

- There is an increased knowledge of the direct relationship and linkage between one group's output and the effect it has on another work group's input (and thus their eventual output).

- The relationships between work groups are much clearer; in particular, the communication lines are more clearly understood by workers and managers alike.

- The opportunity to measure each output is clearly defined, and thus the "whole boat" of the business can be enhanced. When Work Group Analysis is combined with Business Unit Analysis (on which it is based) and analysis at both the Process and Individual level, major business improvements can be anticipated.

Now that all major outputs have been defined and the direction of the business is well known, it is time to go to the third level of business, which is often thought of as "work." This third level is the range of processes as used by individuals and teams under the facilitation of individual managers.

CHAPTER 6

APPLYING THE LANGUAGE OF WORK TO PROCESSES

In this chapter we will expand the application of the Language of Work from the Business Unit, Work Group, and Individual levels to the Process level. Processes are the procedural events carried out by individuals or work groups to produce outputs. As with other levels of the Business Sphere, processes can be diagrammed, explained, managed, measured, and improved most effectively through using the Language of Work. Much of this effectiveness comes from an expanded view of what a process truly is. More traditional thinking has viewed process as merely a set of steps to be followed. The Language of Work recognizes that processes of the Business Sphere are composed of inputs, conditions, the process element, outputs, consequences, and feedback.*

After changing the organization chart (i.e., rearranging, creating, and eliminating work groups) or the leadership of a business unit, changing process is probably the most common way of trying to improve a business. At first glance, changing process makes more sense than changing either the organization chart or the leadership, but there is one very important thing to consider before contemplating changing processes: It is inadvisable to change the process before measuring the output(s) the process is designed to achieve. That old saying "If it works, don't fix it!" fully applies to process: Don't change it unless you find out that something is wrong with the output. This is important to emphasize because many continuous improvement techniques are unwittingly used to measure and change work processes before the overall output is examined. For instance, workers and managers are taught to do a lot of measurements to identify problems with process and fix them before examining the existing satisfaction with the output. Also, the measurement of an output should be a true measure of the output rather than merely someone's opinion that there is something wrong with the output or the process. This is why doing a Busi-

---

* To differentiate the use of the word process in the context of the four major levels of the Business Sphere (Business Unit, Work Group, Process, and Individual) from process as one of the six work elements (inputs, conditions, outputs, process, consequences, and feedback) the latter will be designated as process element.

ness Unit Analysis *before* doing a Process Analysis is so important. Remember: DE-FINE AUSTRALIA FIRST, that is, define the goal first. In this case, the first goal is defining business outputs and the level of satisfaction with them. The goal of business should not be process change.

This chapter will focus on the three basic types of processes—product, service, and knowledge—and the three ways in which they flow in a business. We will see how the Language of Work, through work diagrams, can be applied to product and service processes. Then, we will see how to measure and improve product and service processes. You will also learn a rather unique application of the Language of Work related to using *knowledge* processes. Finally, we will look at systematic processes, which increase effectiveness and efficiency in the workplace.

THE THREE TYPES OF PROCESSES

Product Processes

Product processes lead to tangible product outputs (material things). The production line is a common product process. Product processes may be human-led or machine-led. Usually, the process is readily observed and defined, and its efficiency and effectiveness can be easily changed if attended to. The human element, if involved, is most often improved by a variety of motivational interventions, although skill enhancements may be used to make some improvements. For example, improving the production line in an auto assembly plant is not mainly a case of enhancing the skill of the work force. The work force, unless brand new, already knows how to "assemble." However, making the individual worker a part of a well-functioning team is usually far more effective in bringing about improvements—a kind of motivational intervention. The Saturn Corporation has certainly proved this, even though software and hardware technologies have played major roles as well.

Traditionally, industrial engineering has played a key role in improving product processes. It has enjoyed a notable degree of success with time studies, streamlining, work simplification, facilities layout, and the like, and its approaches are worth knowing; nonetheless, its preoccupation with micro analysis has kept major business improvements from happening. Using the Language of Work in conjunction with Business Unit and Work Group Analysis can help us see the bigger picture of human performance. It is when people play a larger or dominant role in a business, as in service processes, that the Performance Paradigm is most useful. The best approach is to apply the work language to product processes to improve them first; then consider the industrial engineering tools and techniques. How to do this is covered in the following description of service processes.

Service Processes

Service processes also usually result in tangible outputs (such as documentation), but machines and tools are not used as a major part of the process. Workers may use computers and pencil and paper, but these are extensions of the human mind, not machines that stamp out parts in an automated assembly line. Service processes that do not result in tangible outputs often fulfill psychological and physical needs. For example, there are professionals who use processes to produce positive attitudes, understanding, or sensations. These would include those engaged in religion, therapy, counseling, and the like.

Service processes are usually fairly complex. For example, in our sample engineering business, the processes of producing engineering designs, services, and written proposals are complex. Engineering, as an overall process, is very complex. The number of people involved, with varying talents and temperaments and experience, is extensive and hard to control. This is not exactly like pulling a lever to stamp out a part, as in a product process. In service processes we rely on numerous individuals to "do their part"—to understand what must be done—and (as if that were not enough) these individuals can choose whether to do so and can vary the degree of participation. Generally we do not have to worry about the temperament or motivation of a machine, but the human machine is another thing to reckon with.

Now, the complexity of service processes is not new news! What may be *new* news is that those involved in service processes cannot accurately tell you, other than through the technical language of their job, how they do what they do. Can your fellow workers and managers tell you what they do in a common work language that you and others understand? They may be able to tell you what they are supposed to produce as an output (e.g., a written proposal), but having them agree on the exact process used to produce it and working in a timely, cooperative way to achieve it is another matter. And even when they can agree among themselves, how often does another work group or individual or manager have a similar understanding of that same process? Does John, the CAD engineer, understand and appreciate Lee's job as a proposal writer? Does Monica, the trainer, understand and appreciate either John's or Lee's process? If you do not think these are really problems in communication, just ask a proposal writer for his or her opinion on how well a typical project-manager engineer understands the process and timing needs of a proposal writer. Or ask the print shop if the proposal writer understands the printing process and its timing requirements. Ask a trainer if he or she gets much respect from an engineer. These answers would be quite different if each work group had a common work language in order to understand one another's process, for their communication and collaborative efforts to produce a common output (e.g., a finished "excellent proposal") would be so much better.

Knowledge Processes

Knowledge processes are designed to result in outputs that are ideas and decisions. In business, knowledge processes are most often associated with either decision making or problem solving. These may be used by individuals, such as managers and workers, or teams. A team working together to answer a question such as "How should we develop a business development plan for our business?" would need to use a knowledge process. Without a process of this kind, teams and individuals are left to their own devices. It is not uncommon, for instance, to see a group in a typical problem-solving meeting floundering around in search of a process their group can use to accomplish the assigned task.

The most commonly used knowledge process in business is a general discussion. Usually this is merely an individual or group "contemplation" based on prior experience, rather than a systematic process; people do not repeat the process so that they learn how to process better the next time. Typically a group will simply start to discuss their individual perceptions of, and experience with, the "problem" and out of this arrive at some decision based on their collective logic. Often these groups jump to solutions or fail to arrive at any viable solution. Is this a good way to process? Does it get us the best answers or solutions? At best, it is inefficient; at worst, it is ineffective.

It is true that, as a knowledge process, group discussion is often better (although slower) than individual contemplation because it naturally takes into account more points of view. But this does not mean that the output is necessarily a good one, and on average the outcomes are not as good as they would be if more systematic means were used to arrive at the output. When we have a systematic process, we have a defined process that can be successfully repeated and applied again and again to assure greater success in arriving at effective answers and solutions. We need a process we can learn to improve with continued use, one that is "performance-based," such as a process based on the syntax of the Language of Work.

The work matrix application tool is particularly useful for knowledge processes. It matches closely the work diagram and other work application tools used to analyze and improve business units, work groups, and individuals; therefore, using the work language to problem-solve does not require learning a new set of skills that differ substantially from those we have already covered in the analysis of the business unit, work groups, and individuals. It is one work language that can be applied to all work applications, including knowledge processes for decision making and problem solving.

PROCESS FLOW

The first way process flows is within a work group; this is the *overall process* (OP) for that work group. For example, our Engineering work group has an overall engineering process it follows (which we will see later in Figure 6.5). Virtually every work group has an overall process within which it functions. In Monica's Training work group the overall process will be called Performance Technology. In Lee's Proposal Development work group it might be called the Proposal Development process.

Within every work group's overall process (OP), there reside several *individual processes* (IP) that are used to produce each kind of output. For example, John, the CAD engineer, uses a certain kind of individual process to produce his engineering drawings. In like manner, Monica uses an IP—called Instructional Technology—to produce the training program output of the Training work group. Lee uses an IP to develop written proposals, another IP to develop cost proposals, and still other IPs to produce the oral presentation and qualification description outputs that are a part of the Proposal Development work group. It is important to note that all IPs must be linked to the overall process (OP) of which they are a part. More on the latter will be illustrated when we look at some specific examples.

The third kind of process flow occurs between work groups. These are called *shared processes* (SP). Work shared between several work groups, such as the following work groups working on a proposal, exemplifies shared process.

Work Group	Function or Process
Proposal Development	Writes the proposal
Engineering	Provides technical and cost input
Legal	Reviews contractual language
Printing	Prints the proposal document
Training	Supports oral presentation practice

It will be useful to draw out the differences and similarities between the OP, IP, and SP processes for the purpose of making business improvements. Later, we will use the example of the various work groups in the sample engineering business to develop the importance of the difference in process flow.

For all three kinds of process flow (OP, IP, SP), we will be defining inputs, conditions, process element, outputs, consequences, and feedback according to the work-diagram application tool. For product processes, the specifics of a work diagram are easily defined and delineated. Key considerations in business improvement of product processes within the process usually involve such things as timing, quality control, and avoidance of rejects. By contrast, in the case of service processes, the work diagram is a little harder to define because individuals and teams are involved in executing the process, thus compounding the problems in making improvements. As might be expected, when we compare service processes within a work group to those between work groups, the problems of human interaction are compounded further. For example, people in one work group can and do ignore or let slide the needs of another work group, and for many reasons. As previously noted, a print-shop work group is often taken advantage of by other work groups who bring their outputs (i.e., the things they want printed) to the print shop too late, then insist that it be done and that their output is certainly more important than another work group's output currently in the shop. This kind of stress between work groups sharing processes can be very hard on a business unit. The point is, in general, more attention needs to be paid to the human element of work flow processes *between* work groups than *within* work groups. The Language of Work can be applied to reduce stress levels.

This completes the introduction to processes. As with Business Unit and Work Group Analysis, in Process Analysis we will be looking at the development of the work diagram and the related definition and use of performance questions to improve processes. This will round out our use of the Language of Work to improve the four levels of the Business Sphere.

USING THE WORK DIAGRAM APPROACH TO PROCESS ANALYSIS

As we learned in both Business Unit and Work Group Analysis, the order in which we define the elements of the Language of Work to create a work diagram is critical. Therefore, in analyzing process, we will build the process work diagrams in the following sequence:

First: Define, in order, the outputs, inputs, conditions, and consequences.

Second: Define the process element within the process.

Third: Define feedback.

We will first build a typical IP work diagram for an individual, understanding that *individual* in this case may mean several individuals (e.g., several trainers) using the same process. We will use John, the CAD engineer, as our example. Then we will focus on the related OP work diagram of the Engineering work group of which John is a part. Finally, we will look at Lee's Proposal Development work group and see how Engineering, Training, and Legal relate as shared processes (SP) to the Proposal Development process. In doing so, we will be able to see how we can relate these process work diagrams to show process flow relationships in the form of overall process (OP), individual processes (IP), and shared processes (SP). This is important not only to ensure that role relationships are clearly understood, but so we can measure these relationships for quality improvement (such as is commonly the aim of continuous improvement, TQM processes).

Processes for Individuals—IP

Processes produce outputs. Therefore, if you want to know what process you need to define for any individual or work group, you need look no further than the outputs the work group is "chartered" to produce. These were defined during the analysis of the Work Group Analysis (Chapter 5). For illustrative purposes let us see where John's engineering drawings output originated from and what process needs to be defined.

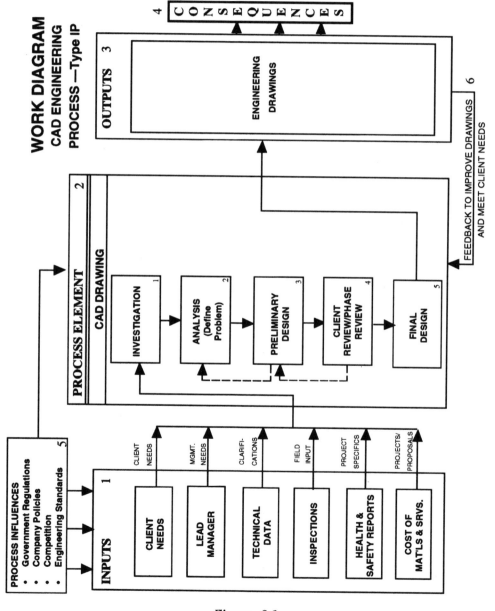

Figure 6.1

Outputs

Of course, John's output, as with any output, originated from the analysis of the business during Business Unit Analysis. In his case, he is part of the Engineering work group, and when we define the outputs for the Engineering work group, we see that engineering drawings is one of the major outputs of the work group, as well as of the business unit.

All outputs should be able to be traced (cascaded) through the entire business at all four levels—Business Unit, Work Group, Process, and Individual. The essence of diagramming any process is, therefore, to first know and define outputs—to DEFINE AUSTRALIA FIRST.

Figure 6.1 shows the complete IP for John's job responsibility of producing engineering drawings. In showing how the IP is developed, the first thing that would be specified are the outputs, as shown below.

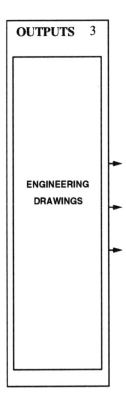

Once the output has been identified for the process, the other parts of the work diagram would be identified and placed in the diagram. Although the individual elements of the IP work diagram will be shown as they are described, you should also refer to Figure 6.1 throughout the following description in order to see the overall context of the work diagram. Note that the elements of work are listed and described in the preferred order in which they should be identified and defined.

Inputs

Inputs typically come from a variety of sources. As you have learned, one source is the client who requests the output. John's clients are typically external clients who request, through RFPs, specific drawings to meet their needs.

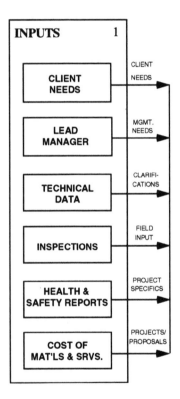

Other inputs for John's IP include specific input from his manager, technical data provided by the client or obtained internally, inspections that John or others make out in the field, factors related to health and safety reports, and the cost of materials and services.

Conditions

All of the inputs and process are influenced by certain conditions that have been specified in the box labeled "Process Influences."

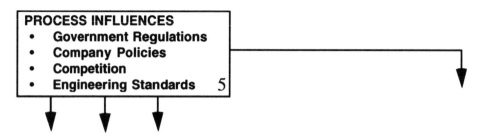

PROCESS INFLUENCES
- **Government Regulations**
- **Company Policies**
- **Competition**
- **Engineering Standards** 5

As is often the case in business, these conditions emanate from inside policies and procedures and outside government regulations. For example, the process in Figure 6.1 would be influenced by a government regulation regarding design standards, as well as by environmental regulations that must be included in the design. These conditions may be written more specifically as the job need dictates. For illustrative purposes, the specification of conditions has been intentionally generic.

Consequences

The consequences are not shown on the diagram but as a separate list. Since the drawings are for specific outputs that will be utilized to construct some physical structure, device, or other item, the consequences are fairly simple. Here is a list of typical consequences for this sample:

- A design with which the client is satisfied and that meets their budget requirements

- A design esthetically pleasing to the environment it will be used in

- John's personal satisfaction of a job well done

- The satisfaction of John's manager

Process Element

Now that we have defined the inputs, conditions, and consequences of the output(s), the next major step is to develop the process element for the IP in the work diagram. The process element you choose to define may be a step-by-step process or it may have parallel and simultaneous steps. The examples provided in this book use linear steps for the sake of simplicity. As shown on the next page and in Figure 6.1, there are five steps to the CAD Drawing process element.

Notice that this particular process element—CAD Drawing— is very systematic, an important feature in the total picture of improving a business. Shortly, more will be said about systematic processes.

Feedback

The final step of Process Analysis is to define feedback. On the Process level, feedback has four forms. The first three forms of feedback help us learn how to process outputs better. The fourth is shared between work groups. It is best to prepare for all these forms of feedback rather than simply wait for them. Preparedness makes us more conscious of the work at hand and can increase the quality of our performance. We're more apt to receive positive feedback, and even if the feedback is less than complimentary, we are in a better position to respond in a constructive way.

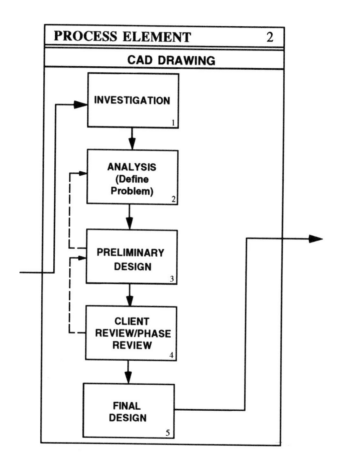

Although it is contrary to human nature to go out of our way to seek "trouble" or to assert ourselves when we are shy, we need to encourage, even demand, voluntary feedback from internal clients in the Business Sphere. One way to increase the likelihood of feedback occurring is to actually plan for it—a practice that is beginning to increase as the TQM movement becomes more widely accepted in business. In the usual TQM context, feedback is obtained largely through the mechanism of measurement. Measurement is also a key element in the Business Sphere approach addressed ment. Measurement is also a key element in the Business Sphere approach addressed in this book. However, in taking the Business Sphere approach, we also want to emphasize planning for feedback as part of our implementation of processes, and we should provide opportunities for managers and workers to see that we value feedback as a positive consequence of their work.

Shown below and in Figure 6.1 are two examples of planned feedback loops. They occur in the process element between Steps 2 and 3, and Steps 3 and 4. Others could be included, but these are known by business experience to be particularly critical for this specific process.

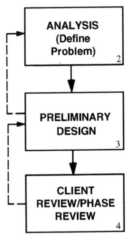

Each feedback loop has an arrow to indicate direction, although the most effective feedback is really a two-way communication from sender to receiver and back again. For example, the client review and phase review in Step 4 will provide valuable feedback information that could change the preliminary design of an engineering drawing so that the output will be more favorable to the client. In a similar way, working on the preliminary design in Step 3 may reveal the need to make certain alterations to the initial analysis of the problem in Step 2. Since process-element steps are often completed in conjunction with workers and management, feedback is necessary in order to keep everyone informed. This kind of information may well change in some way the work they are doing. At a minimum, it helps others feel that you are keeping them informed, even when the information being fed back doesn't alter their work.

We also see in this example a second kind of feedback. This feedback is not so much concerned with the "immediate" output as it is with information that would enhance a step in the process element itself, thus ultimately enhancing the output. For example, in Step 4, if we involve the external client in the review—a kind of preliminary tryout—the feedback they provide would be very useful in assuring that the drawing is headed in the right direction. This is called *developmental* feedback, and it always involves the client. In a sense, we are testing the output we are processing on the subject who will be receiving it. In addition to getting a more accurate assessment of our processing than we would get if we waited until the end of the process, we also involve the client in a way that makes them feel valued. We are keeping them informed. This is the kind of feedback that clients love to receive.

There is a third form of feedback in Figure 6.1, labeled "Feedback to Improve Drawings and Meet Client Needs."

This particular feedback reminds us to seek out information from the user of the training output as to how any element of the work diagram for this process unit can be made better. In this example, the client receives the engineering drawings. Do we simply give the drawings to the client and wait to be paid? Or do we ask the client how he or she liked the drawings and whether they are up to the desired standards? From the results of this kind of measurement, we feed back information to those who executed the process element, provided the input, controlled the conditions, and/or influenced the consequences. Revisions would be made to improve processing the output in order to assure satisfying this client and other clients in the future. In large measure, we are trying to assure that the current and future clients will want to return for further work with us. We are also trying to make our process more systematic by learning what we did right and wrong and then fixing what needs fixing. This is deliberate and not left to chance. It is directed at improving the process element, and not just the individual who gains experience.

There is a fourth form of feedback—timely feedback—that relates to processes between work groups. This will be illustrated when we discuss processes shared by work groups, known as shared processes (SP).

Figure 6.2, an IP diagram for Monica's position as a trainer, is provided for further study (see following page). You may wish to review the different work elements in this process, giving special attention to the different forms of feedback. Note in particular Step 5, Tryout and Measurement. This is an excellent illustration of developmental feedback.

Overall Process for Work Groups—OP

Work groups traditionally reflect the process that makes them unique; individuals are organized together as a work group to use that process. For example, engineers use an engineering process and become an engineering work group. Sometimes work group organization makes sense, and sometimes it does not. Whether the work group contains members from the same dicipline or from a variety of work functions, there should be an overall process (OP) that defines how the work group will do their work.

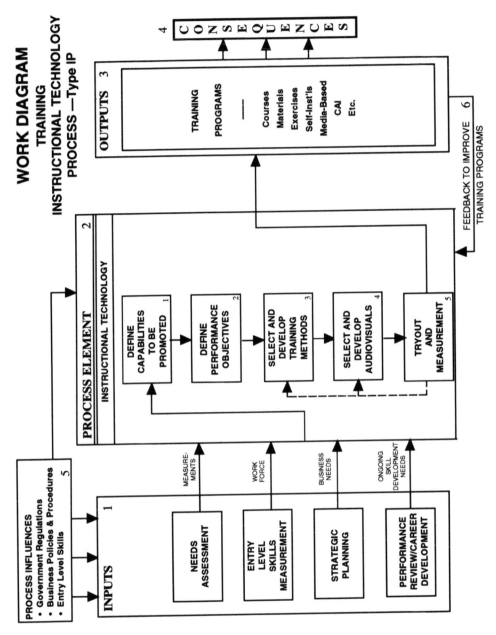

Figure 6.2

A typical overall process is Engineering. Thus, while John, our CAD engineer, uses his own individual process to do CAD drawings (see Figure 6.1), he does so within an overall process (OP), illustrated in the work diagram for Engineering in Figure 6.3. In like manner, Figure 6.4 is an OP for a training work group, within which Monica's IP (Figure 6.2) as a trainer would fit. Note that the OP always sub-

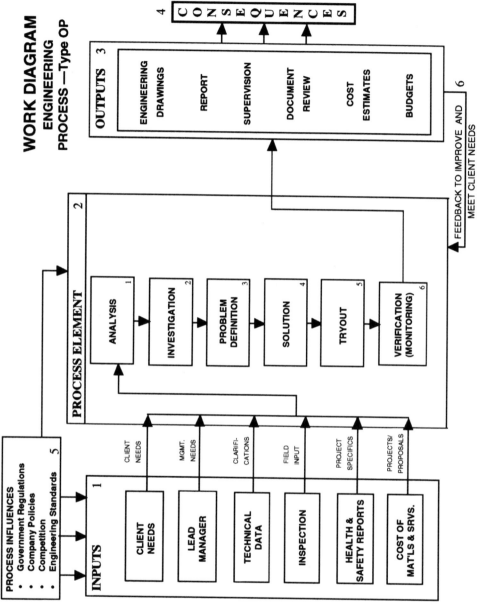

Figure 6.3

sumes within it, and is consistent with, a variety of IPs used by various individuals. The distinction between OPs and IPs is this:

- OPs define the process of work groups.

- IPs define the process of individuals.

- Usually, there are several IPs within an OP.

Remember: OPs for a business must be defined prior to IPs for individuals. This is because OPs are defined relative to major outputs that the business wants to produce. Thus, the Engineering OP in Figure 6.3 was defined to achieve one or more of the major business unit outputs, in this case, reports, engineering design, and certain services. The IP for a CAD engineer will be defined after the OP in order to help the Engineering work group achieve one of its outputs, engineering drawings. Other IPs would also be defined to help achieve other outputs of Engineering, including reports, supervision, document review, cost estimates, and budgets.

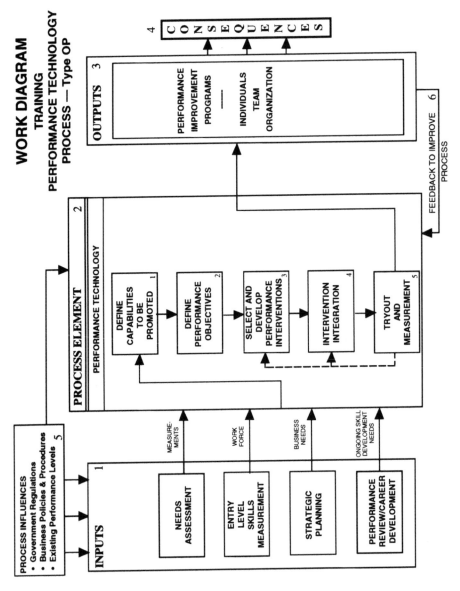

Figure 6.4

To see how the Engineering OP work diagram was developed, as usual we begin with output. The outputs in Figure 6.3, as shown below, are the outputs of the Engineering work group. Engineering in the original business-unit work diagram, Figure 4.1, preceded the Project Management work group (see page 101).

Because our sample business is an engineering business, quite naturally the Engineering work group would be concerned with virtually all the major outputs of the business. The following display illustrates that the outputs listed in the Engineering OP are the same as the outputs for the business unit (Figure 4.1), with the exception that other, more specific outputs are also listed for Engineering.

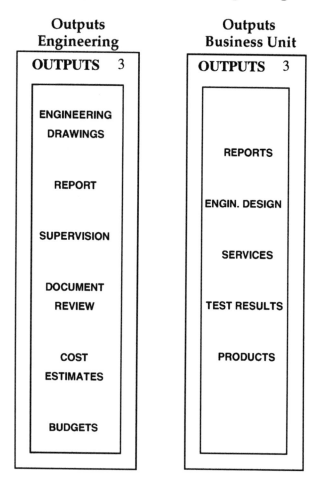

Once the outputs have been defined for an OP, the following order is used to define the remaining work elements of the OP work diagram: inputs, conditions, consequences, process element, and feedback. As these work elements have been sufficiently described in previous chapters, in the discussion of work diagramming and analysis on the Business Unit, Work Group, and Individual levels, they will not be described in detail here. We will later return to the OP for Engineering and see how the Process Element section is an excellent example of a systematic process.

We can see once again that if we trace the outputs throughout a business, applying the Language of Work, we can help managers and workers—and very importantly, the business itself—better understand work and communicate more clearly. In this case, they can see why we have overall processes (OP) and where their individual processes (IP) fit within them. Next, we will see where processes are shared with other work groups. We call these, quite naturally, shared processes (SP).

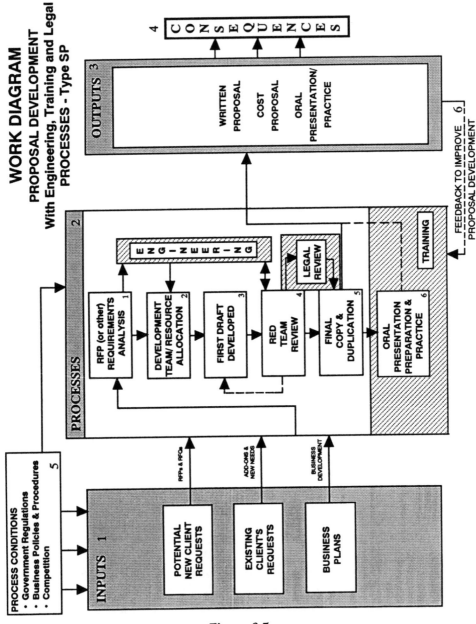

Figure 6.5

Shared Process Between Work Groups—SP

Figure 6.5 is a SP work diagram for the Proposal Development work group and related work groups of our sample engineering business. Please review the diagram's sections for the six work elements—outputs, inputs, conditions, consequences, process element, and feedback—before reading the following description.

Notice that in this particular process work diagram, the work relationship with other work groups has been included. These are the relationships of Proposal Development to the Legal, Engineering, and Training work groups. Each work group having a relationship to Proposal Development is shown in the shaded, hashed-line areas. For instance, we can see in the following that during the process element, Lee, the proposal writer, performs RFP Requirements Analysis (Step 1), Development Team/Resource Allocation (Step 2), and Red Team Review (Step 4) with the Engineering work group.

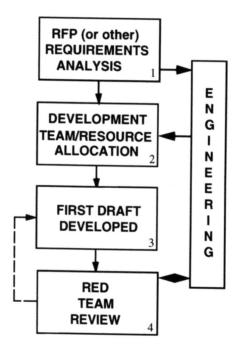

In Step 6 of the Proposal Development process, Lee shares with Monica, the trainer, certain activities when developing an oral presentation and practice session. This is shown in Figure 6.5 by the following:

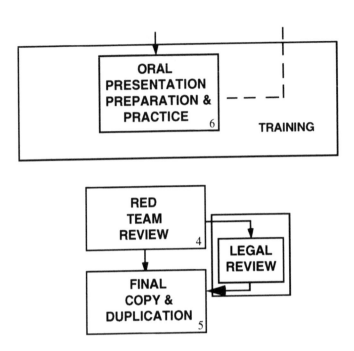

Finally, we can also see a shared relationship with the Legal work group. By diagramming and showing these kinds of relationships, we can address the nature and scope of the relationships, looking in particular for needed improvements.

Before we move on to a discussion of measurement, it is important to take a look at the fourth type of feedback that typically exists around processes and between work groups: timely feedback. Its distinguishing feature is that its effectiveness depends on when it is provided. The lack of timely feedback is the source of problems between work groups that share processes, such as those exemplified in Figure 6.5. For instance, the Legal department will provide substantive feedback on the technical/legal issues of a written proposal; however, if their feedback is not solicited (or returned) in a timely manner, neither their task nor output (as input to Proposal Development) will be what it should be. This type of feedback, like the others, needs to be measured and attended to if the process is to be efficient and effective.

This special emphasis on timeliness in planning and assuring feedback is made here because timeliness is so violated in business. Individual work groups should regard their own processes in the context of the overall effectiveness of the shared process they have in common with other groups and individuals. It should be the aim of all work groups to work for the common good of the business unit's outputs. When individual work groups only consider and act for their own welfare, problems result. Therefore, one of the performance questions that management must plan to specify and measure in relation to process is the timeliness of feedback between work groups. This may seem obvious, but ill-timed feedback—feedback that is neither planned, expected, measured, nor reinforced with appropriate consequences—is one of the bigger failures of modern business when it comes to process.

MEASURING AND IMPROVING PROCESSES

To prepare yourself for the topic of measuring processes, review the various work diagrams that have been used as illustrations for individuals, work groups, processes, and the business unit. As you look at these work diagrams, recall the description of how the outputs (and other elements) of the diagram should first be measured. Now, what does the review indicate to you about measuring processes?

Perhaps the first thing you learned from the review is that if we have measured the outputs at the Business Unit, Work Group, or Individual levels, then the outputs for the process have been measured. For example, compare the previously illustrated outputs for two engineering processes and the output for John's engineering job:

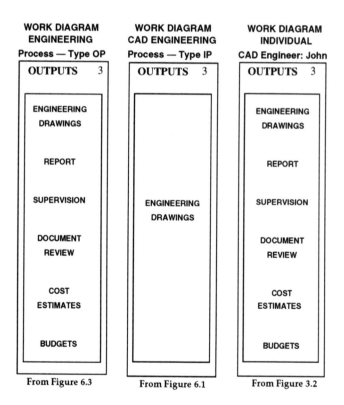

WORK DIAGRAM ENGINEERING	WORK DIAGRAM CAD ENGINEERING	WORK DIAGRAM INDIVIDUAL
Process — Type OP	Process — Type IP	CAD Engineer: John
OUTPUTS 3	OUTPUTS 3	OUTPUTS 3
ENGINEERING DRAWINGS		ENGINEERING DRAWINGS
REPORT		REPORT
SUPERVISION	ENGINEERING DRAWINGS	SUPERVISION
DOCUMENT REVIEW		DOCUMENT REVIEW
COST ESTIMATES		COST ESTIMATES
BUDGETS		BUDGETS
From Figure 6.3	From Figure 6.1	From Figure 3.2

Notice the same outputs show up in each work diagram. With the exception of the IP process, each of the outputs would have been measured at one of these levels. Therefore, the first lesson in measuring processes is to make sure that the outputs have been (or will be) measured first. This is another instance of DEFINE AUSTRALIA FIRST. Once the outputs have been measured and any problem with one or more has been identified, you are ready to measure the related inputs, conditions, process, consequences, and feedback. With an understanding that outputs of a process have been measured, we will look at two aspects of process improvement:

1. Measuring the work elements of the process

2. Personal assessment and adjustment of process

Measuring the Work Elements of Processes

Measuring the various work elements within a process is not significantly different from measuring the work elements previously described for the business unit, work groups, and individuals. We still need to know how the conditions support the process. We need to see that the inputs meet standards and are ready in a timely way for processing. We want to assure that positive consequences are provided as incentives to processing correctly and on time. We need to make sure that feedback is solicited from the client when the output is delivered. It is in the process element of a process that we need to provide some additional detail. We will use the SP of proposal development as the point of reference in the description that follows. This SP process is shown in Figure 6.5; the process element is reproduced below for your reference as the following description is given.

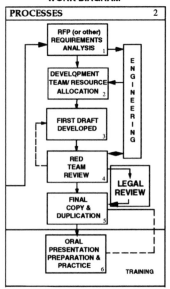

PROCESS ELEMENT
OF PROPOSAL DEVELOPMENT
WORK DIAGRAM

Areas to measure within the process element include:

1. Measuring the output of each step in the process element.

We have already measured the major outputs of the process and have either found these outputs satisfactory or have indicated the need for improvement. For example, one of the major outputs of the SP proposal development process is the written proposal. Suppose we have measured and found that something seems to be wrong with the written proposals. Clients consistently say that the written proposals are not sufficiently addressing their direct needs as expressed in the RFP (Step 1 of the process element). So what do we do? We know that we will want to measure the inputs, conditions, consequences, and client feedback. What about measuring the process element?

When we measure the process element, the first thing we will want to measure is the output of each step in the process—remember, DEFINE AUSTRALIA FIRST. You have probably noticed that each time we go further into the various levels of the business, from business unit to the individual, we always measure output first. In many respects, measuring the outputs of various steps of a process element is the last output to be measured. We have cascaded our way to the ultimate source of a work problem as far as output is concerned. For example, the fourth step in the proposal development process is the Red Team Review. What outputs of this step would we be likely to measure?

A Red Team Review is a process-element step during which a group of internal experts (i.e., engineers) role-play the role of an external client for whom the proposal is being written. The Red Team takes a constructively critical look at a draft of the written proposal at an early stage to make suggestions on how the proposal may be improved. Their specific outputs would include such things as (1) a description of the value of the content, schedule, and resource allocations, (2) where the proposal addresses what the client asked for in the Request for Proposal (RFP), and (3) other technical and sales requirements. To measure this step of the process, these outputs need to be reviewed as useful information on which the proposal writer can base adjustments. If the Red Team is not providing useful information to the proposal writer to improve the quality of the proposal, then the Red Team Review step needs to be revised. This evaluation will help to improve the steps of a process element.

Now suppose that the proposal writer ignores what the Red Team suggests. This provides a lead-in to the second major aspect of a process element to measure: feedback.

2. Measure the feedback between steps in the process element.

This is one of the classic areas for a breakdown in processing. Sometimes feedback is not provided or, when given, is ignored or not understood. It is important, therefore, to measure for feedback between steps in a process element.

In the proposal development process, we notice that there is a feedback loop from Step 4 to Step 3—feedback from the Red Team to be used by the proposal writer to revise the first draft in Step 3. If we measure the outputs of the Red Team Review and find that they are satisfactory, yet the proposal document still poses problems because it does not fulfill the client's specific requests, we can measure to see if the proposal writer has responded to the specific suggestions of the Red Team Review (among other things). If not, the response to the feedback needs to be fixed. A similar measure would be made of whether the proposal writer has responded to the Legal Review feedback that makes its way from the Legal work group into Step 5 of the process element.

3. Eliminating or re-engineering steps of the process element.

One of the things we typically attempt to improve is the efficiency of individual steps in a process element. In today's popular vernacular, it is common to think in terms of re-engineering the steps of a process. Essentially this means determining which steps in the process element *add value* to the process. Those that do not are eliminated—or at least revised. Obviously, careful standards must be applied as to what truly adds value.

For example, we can evaluate the extent to which training is able to add value to the work of the proposal writer in developing Step 6 of the process element, labeled "Oral Presentation Preparation & Practice." We might determine that over time the proposal writer has received sufficient training, that he has observed so many presentations and has practiced the skill of structuring oral presentations so often that he no longer needs the assistance of the Training work group. Thus, training no longer adds value to the overall process; it is therefore eliminated as a result of this analysis, and Step 6 either eliminated or revised.

Personal Assessment and Adjustment of Process

Although performance questions provide us with the most reliable means of determining where work improvements are needed, other approaches may be used in concert with formal measurement. Personal assessment is one such alternative—and, in general, it is not a stranger to the workplace. Workers and managers personally assess work situations on an everyday basis in the execution of their work, and they adjust their processes accordingly, to compensate for the dynamics—the seemingly ever-changing environment—of the workplace: A client decides he needs his order now; the production department nearly grinds to a halt under a sudden rush of orders; John gets sick and cannot deliver a drawing to the project manager when promised. The Language of Work, when applied to personal assessment and process improvement, can greatly aid workers and managers in evaluating situations like these and making adjustments to ensure the timeliness and quality of outputs.

In the context of improving processes, personal assessment is the determination that one or more or both of the following problems are likely to develop: that a delay will occur in getting an output completed on time, or that the output will be completed at a level of quality that is lower than the standard. The worker or manager may realize this on his or her own by paying careful attention to any process element problems, to the availability and quality of inputs, or to adverse conditions that present themselves. It is also possible that someone such as an external or internal client may cause the delay or make a request that the process be sped up so they will receive the output sooner.

Process can be adjusted in a number of ways. Eliminating steps, speeding up the execution of steps, negotiating quality standards, using technology, adding input resources, and negotiating changes in conditions are all possible forms of adjustment. To understand how we might make adjustments such as these, let us pose a problem for the Proposal Development process depicted in Figure 6.5. Suppose a client has requested a written and cost proposal on an engineering project, and suddenly wants the engineering business to submit the proposal five days earlier than originally indicated. What could be done to adjust the process?

One of the first adjustments would be adding additional resources, something many businesses do when faced with a problem like this. Among the specific resource adjustments: more proposal writers could be added, overtime could be authorized, and the Proposal Writing department could bring in additional typists, graphic artists, and other specialists. Another adjustment would be to eliminate (or modify in some way) Step 4—the Red Team Review. This would cut down the steps of the process in this instance. On the flip side, some members of the Red Team group could be involved in the actual writing of the proposal. Either adjustment is designed to speed up the process. It is possible that using technology would speed up the process even more. This adjustment might involve using computer-generated graphics, instead of hand-prepared graphics, produced either in-house or by an outside firm.

Some of the more interesting adjustments in process involve changing conditions and standards. Of course, processes that are designed to lead to exacting standards or that require strict adherence to conditions may not be able to take advantage of these adjustments—medical outputs, exacting equipment standards, and so forth. But there are outputs that can be modified. For instance, one can imagine negotiating with a client who wants the proposal earlier to see what aspects of the written proposal could be delayed or eliminated—for example, resumes on proposed personnel for the project could be provided at some future date. A change in standards, such as budget breakdowns, might allow for changes in the format of the written proposal that were originally imposed by the client.

MAKING PROCESSES SYSTEMATIC

A good process should produce an acceptable output every time it is used. Why doesn't it? Well, we know that the human element can be a significant contributor to varying outputs. People get tired, lose their motivation, have personal problems, and so on. These are subjects of human psychology. The Language of Work can help improve consistent quality output by making processes more systematic.

Systematic processes are characterized by the following:

- A defined set of steps that can be repeatedly applied

- The use of feedback as the steps are applied. This assures adjustments are made to the process element so that it is more effective and efficient

- The use of measurement to make sure the output is satisfactory. Measurement is also used to provide data on which revisions can be based to improve the output before it is finished

- Consistent utilization that improves the process element for the purpose of applying it better the next time

It is important to note that processes are systematic only when all these characteristics are present. For example, virtually all processes have defined steps, but this alone does not make the process highly systematic. In particular, it is the presence of feedback and measurement that often makes a process systematic. As we have already covered feedback in detail, discussing the various kinds of feedback and how they flow in processes, here we will look at feedback in the context of measurement.

Systematic processes may include three important kinds of measurement: measuring output, feedback, and tryout.

1. Systematically measuring output

When we systematically measure output we respond continually to the needs and desires of our clients, be they internal or external. We continuously attend to improving the inputs, conditions, process element, consequences, and feedback, because we want the output to maintain a certain quality standard.

2. *Systematically attending to feedback*

Feedback is a way to keep others informed, as well as a way to collect information for ourselves. Unfortunately, the lack of feedback is one of the principle failures in processing. When we structure feedback as a requirement in processing at specific steps, we make the process more systematic. You will recall that the structured feedback in the Proposal Development process required a legal review. Without the requirement, the output can suffer. By systematically requiring or giving feedback at every critical step in our work, high quality in the output is more assured.

3. *Systematic tryout*

Most, but not all, processes lend themselves to tryout. Tryout is using the intended output on a real or simulated client in order to determine their satisfaction and utilization of the output. For example, the Red Team Review in the Proposal Development process is a kind of tryout. When Monica, the trainer, tries a new training program on a sample group of trainees, tests what they learned, and makes improvements in the training program before it goes to everyone else, she is using a tryout. Tryout can be built into many processes that currently do not employ such a step.

The alternative to a systematic process is a very random walk through the application of processes, from which little learning occurs. As a result, we create new errors rather than improve each time we apply ourselves to the process. Systematic processes are very important to the success of businesses and individuals. The Language of Work, which is itself systematic, can be used to improve nonsystematic processes by helping us define the process-element steps, give attention to measurement, offer feedback, and provide consistent utilization by users.

KNOWLEDGE PROCESSES

Knowledge processes are used daily by managers, individuals, and work groups. Most often these are part of the ongoing daily activities designed to accomplish product and service processes. Improving knowledge processes affords tremendous opportunities for improving many aspects of a business.

Knowledge processes deal with problem solving and decision making. Business is fraught with knowledge processes, making this a key area of business in which improvements can be realized. In applying the Language of Work to these processes, we will mainly address problem or decision situations that call for careful study, rather than focus on the more simple knowledge processes where common sense or experience tells one what to do.

WORK MATRIX: PROBLEM-SOLVING EXAMPLE

	INPUT	CONDITIONS	PROCESS	OUTPUT	CONSEQUENCES	FEEDBACK
WHAT EXISTS	1. Existing job descriptions 2. Job Task List of past performance 3. Interview with others who know of worker's performance	1. Schedule for reviews 2. Beginning of employment/ six months/ tied to salary review, etc. 3. Documentation	1. Worker & manager use "Performance Review" Form.	1. Completed X Corp. "Employee Review Program" Booklet 2. Review of past (six to twelve month) performance	1. Worker understands past performance and why some opportunities were not feasible. 2. Supervisor understands past performance achieved and reasons why opportunities for others were not possible.	1. Provide past performance reviews on specific tasks related to each accountability from supervisor and others 2. Job satisfaction in general 3. Periodic progress discussions during the year on current performance
WHAT SHOULD EXIST	1. Projection of job task needs 2. Career development objectives	1. Career development opportunities	1. Need to reflect "Performance Plan" for next six months 2. Need to tie the job responsibilities to those in job description(s)	1. Performance plan for next six to twelve months 2. Career development opportunities that are tied to specific job responsibilities of a new job (description)	1. Understand areas for future improvement in present job 2. Understand what job responsibilities to work on for career development 3. Understand the relationship of their job responsibilities to other jobs they work with, for, or might grow towards	1. Periodic progress discussions during the year on career development
SOLUTION(S)	1. Career Day: "Somebody else's job" 2. Career Book 3. "Job Lunch"	NONE	1. Mgr. and associates discuss future performance plan for specific responsibilities tied to current job description. 2. They list new job accountabilities and how to achieve them.	1. Expansion of the existing form to include a plan for the next six to twelve months for current job responsibilities. 2. A new section of the performance review plan that incorporates (a) new job responsibilities to work on, (b) specification of what job the responsibility relates to, and (c) plan for achieving the responsibility over next six to twelve months.	1. Employee's sense that company is proactive in career development and job planning. 2. Reduce turnover 3. Meet future job needs 4. Increase morale	1. Add career development feedback discussions 2. Provide progress reports to Human Resources on career development for potential job vacancy needs

Figure 6.6

Figure 6.6 illustrates the use of the work-matrix application tool for problem solving using the six work elements. In this particular example, a problem-solving quality improvement team was charged with devising a way for planning future work while also planning career development opportunities for employees within a performance review system. Using the Language of Work, they created a matrix. On the left end of the matrix, you will find three headings: "What Exists," "What Should Exist," and "Solution(s)."

- **What Exists** includes all information that relates to inputs, conditions, process element, outputs, consequences, and feedback for what currently exists in the business environment. In Figure 6.6, the current situation described is a performance review program between a manager and a worker that centers on a review of job accomplishments over the past six to twelve months. By reading the information across the matrix, you should get a clear picture of what the current situation is for the problem being analyzed. For a problem-solving team, having a clear idea of what currently exists is paramount to determining what should exist.

- **What Should Exist** includes all information that relates to inputs, conditions, process element, outputs, consequences, and feedback for what should exist in the ideal business situation. According to the information entered into the various categories of the work matrix, the new output would have two new features: (1) a performance plan for the next six to twelve months, and (2) a direct tie between responsibilities covered in performance reviews and the worker's current job descriptions, other jobs, and career development opportunities. Related changes, if any, are specified for the six work elements as they relate to the new desired outputs. Note that the outputs are descriptions of desired characteristics. This is because we do not know the form the output solution will take, so we describe its desired characteristics. By contrast, the outputs under "What Exists" are very specific. When a group involved in a problem situation describes all the elements for "What Should Exist," they have a clear idea of what the goal is.

When a problem-solving team has worked through "What Exists" and "What Should Exist," they then have before them a clear picture of the current situation and the ideal situation. Specifications such as these are known as "performance discrepancies" (opportunities) and present a clear picture of what needs solving. What remains is then to arrive at a solution.

- **Solution(s)** represents what will be done to effect the change to a business improvement. In this context, a solution is not just a single answer to the problem; it is a detailed explanation of what needs to be changed in one or more of the work elements. In the usual problem-solving situation, the solution is the new output. In the example, the solution is envisioned as the new form. However, in the Language of Work view, the solution is not just output; rather, one of the nice aspects of the work matrix is that it makes clear what changes are needed in output-related process elements, inputs, conditions, feedback, and consequences. For example, the Career Development Opportunities output, as part of the solution in Figure 6.6, calls for additional inputs.

You can see that the matrix model of problem solving lends structure to group problem-solving discussions. It also requires full exploration of all aspects of what exists, should exist, and the solution itself. When the matrix is put on a white board and used to focus data gathering, problem solving, and decision making, the group typically stays on course rather than straying into random discussions. For knowledge processes, the work matrix is very effective and efficient. It is particularly recommended for more complete and comprehensive business planning—another knowledge process.

BENEFITS OF USING THE LANGUAGE OF WORK ON THE PROCESS LEVEL

Processes represent one of the most frequently examined arenas in which to make business improvements. However, many businesses limit their current thinking of process to the process element. The Language of Work provides a much broader perspective of process, one that includes not only the process element but also inputs, conditions, outputs, consequences, and feedback. This is perhaps the greatest benefit of the Language of Work in relation to process analysis and improvement.

However, as we have learned in this chapter, there are several other benefits of a Language of Work approach to the process level.

- It gives us a way to define individual processes in the context of the overall process used by work groups. Thus, having first defined the overall process, we can ensure that the individual processes used by workers and managers are consistent with the overall process. If we neglect to do this, then the individuals tend to drive the processes of the business, rather than the business determining what processes are best for producing its outputs.

- Once we have defined the overall processes, the Language of Work affords us a way to relate these processes to other work group processes as shared processes. The output of specific steps can be investigated to see where other work groups can be of service in strengthening a step in the process or contributing their own input to the execution of a particular step. Such decisions are simply made easier by using the Language of Work to diagram the shared processes.

- The Language of Work provides us with an orderly way to measure and fix processes. We know to measure the outputs of a process first—to DEFINE AUSTRALIA FIRST. Any output that is not up to standards can then be examined for cause-and-effect factors in the related work elements of that process.

- We can use the Language of Work to improve nonsystematic processes by making them systematic. This is accomplished by defining all six work elements, attending to feedback, and assuring an ongoing measurement of the process outputs and steps in the process element.

- The Language of Work can be applied to knowledge processes, such as problem solving and decision making. It gives us a work matrix tool that is particularly useful in group discussions and individual analysis designed to arrive at business improvement solutions.

We now have seen how the Language of Work can be applied to the four levels of the Business Sphere. In the final chapter we will see how to best introduce this new language into your business.

CHAPTER 7

INTRODUCING THE LANGUAGE OF WORK INTO YOUR BUSINESS SPHERE

In implementing the Language of Work, I discovered early on that workers and managers must initially see the relevance of the work language to themselves and to their relationships with others in the workplace. Originally, when I first developed the Language of Work, I began by showing individuals the entire Business Sphere; then we worked our way from the outside of the Sphere (Business Unit level), through the Work Group and Process levels, and into the center (Individual level). This proved to be too much for most people to absorb and apply. Consequently, I changed my approach and introduced the work language by focusing on the Individual level first. Each individual was asked to define a work diagram for his or her job, and then to share the diagram with other work-group members—just as you were asked to do in Chapter 3. Next, workers and managers learned and practiced other work applications from the paradigms for managers, workers, and teams (Figure 1.3, 1.4, and 1.6, respectively). I found that this modified approach met with far greater success, and it is the approach I now use and recommend. I also recommend that you and others use the Language of Work on the Individual level for at least six to nine months. This establishes a basic level of proficiency and commitment in the use of the work language. Then, from that commitment, the worker and manager will be well prepared to learn and apply the Language of Work at the Business Unit, Work Group, and Process levels.

To introduce the Language of Work into your business, you will be using a work application tool called an implementation plan. There will be two implementation plans, one each for the two-phase approach to introducing the Language of Work. As a result of the implementation plan, your business will attain two overall major consequences that build the desirable Business Sphere: an "informed work force" and a "quality-driven culture."

PHASING-IN THE LANGUAGE OF WORK—THE RECOMMENDED APPROACH

Because it is imperative that individuals see the immediate importance of the language to themselves before a broader application is made to the rest of the business, a two-phase approach to implementation is recommended. Phase 1, "Introducing the Language of Work," focuses on the Individual level of the Business Sphere. Phase 2, "Expanding the Use of the Language of Work," is concerned with implementing the work language on the Process, Work Group, and Business Unit levels of the Business Sphere.

Phase 1: Introducing the Language of Work

Figure 7.1 is an implementation plan for Phase 1. A description of each of the six elements will give you a clear picture of what to do in the initial phase of introducing the Language of Work into your business. As usual, we begin with outputs.

Outputs of Phase 1

In phase 1 we want individual managers, workers, and teams to learn the work language and practice it on themselves. As shown in the outputs of Figure 7.1, this means being able to use the Language of Work for each of the work functions that were listed in the work applications paradigms in Figures 1.3, 1.4, and 1.6 (see Chapter 1). These include such work functions as making task assignments, facilitating work, measuring quality, problem solving, and the like.

Inputs for Phase 1

The inputs for introducing the work language are the job functions. These are the needs of managers and workers that must be fulfilled. As managers, workers, and teams are unable to perform these functions as effectively and efficiently as they should, the business wants the individuals to improve them. Again, these functions are listed in work applications paradigms in Figures 1.3, 1.4, and 1.6.

A second class of inputs is the variety of work application tools that can be used by managers, workers, and teams to help apply the work language to the work functions. As performance aids, they are an important input.

Conditions of Phase 1

There is one specific and one general class of conditions that affect implementation in Phase 1. The specific condition is the Performance Paradigm. In learning and applying the Language of Work, the individuals must fully know what the relationship is between the six elements of work. Without this knowledge, the work language

PHASE 1
IMPLEMENTATION PLAN
INTRODUCING THE LANGUAGE OF WORK
(Individuals)

INPUTS

Job Functions
Work Application Tools

CONDITIONS

Performance Paradigm
Management Commitment

PROCESS

Workshop
Modeling
Coaching

OUTPUT

Improved effectiveness and efficiency in:
- Manager's Work Applications
- Worker's Work Applications
- Team's Work Applications

CONSEQUENCES

Expanded view of work:
- Improved effectiveness and efficiency in work functions
- Buy-in to Language of Work
- Desire for more of the Language of Work
- Improved worker/manager relations

FEEDBACK

Measuring the output—Measured results
Measured process:
- Worker-to-worker feedback
- Manager-to-worker feedback
- Worker-to-manager feedback

Figure 7.1

might be analyzed and applied inappropriately or incompletely. Therefore, the Performance Paradigm is a condition to be adhered to.

The general conditions that affect the use of the Language of Work include the commitment and attitude of management towards the Language of Work. As with any program, process, procedure, or concept, without management support and encouragement, workers and managers will generally not respond.

Process for Phase 1

Of course, many methods can be used to introduce the Language of Work in an organization, but I have primarily used three related interventions: a workshop, modeling, and coaching.

Through a series of individual and group exercises, the workshop introduces and provides in-class practice in the Language of Work. For instance, participants diagram their jobs and share the work diagrams; then, through a series of exercises, they apply the work language to other job functions. In one of the more useful approaches, the individuals learn to apply the various work application tools to several job functions, then demonstrate how they would apply the Language of Work to other job functions. In this way they begin to learn how to use the language to solve a need by themselves, rather than relying on others to tell them how to do each job function.

In the process of training and on the job itself, successful modeling of various job functions is introduced and practiced. For example, in one company a group learned to expand its existing "work application package"—a kind of work-order form and procedure—to include a work-plan application tool based on the Language of Work. Modeling usually takes the form of displaying many examples of different application tools that can be replicated. Also, individuals and teams demonstrate the use of the work language in various functions (i.e., problem solving).

Finally, coaching is used on the job to help individuals meet the specific work applications that confront them. For example, a team is trying to solve a particular problem assigned them. An instructor from the workshop or a consultant provides assistance (coaching) to the team in applying a problem-solving work matrix.

The workshop segment usually takes about three days. The modeling and coaching is provided on an as-needed basis. As previously noted, the overall Phase 1 process of learning, practicing, and applying the Language of Work in a business is recommended to last six to nine months before Phase 2 is initiated.

Consequences of Phase 1

There are several specific consequences of Phase 1, but the overriding consequence is labeled the "expanded view of work"— a topic that will be described later as a major consequence of introducing the Language of Work into your business. The workers, managers, and teams expand their thinking, going from a limited, process-oriented view of work to a definition of work that includes all six elements of work. As such, other specific consequences result, including:

- Improved effectiveness and efficiency in individual and group work functions. This is achieved by using the various work application tools and the different work applications.

- Buy-in to the Language of Work. This is achieved by using and seeing the value of the work language for yourself and others.

- The desire to learn more about the work language. In seeing the positive effects on yourself and others, you can see the potential of its application to other aspects of the business, such as processes, your work group, and the business unit itself.

- Improved worker/manager relations. The Language of Work improves communication between workers and managers.

Feedback in Phase 1

Several versions of feedback are typically employed in Phase 1. These include:

1. Measuring the Outputs—Measured Results

Those responsible for implementing Phase 1 will want to measure to see that individuals are actually able to develop and use the various kinds of work application tools on the job. For instance, are managers talking the work language when doing performance reviews? Are teams using the work matrix to do problem solving? Are workers measuring the quality of their work? These various applications can be measured by surveys completed by workers and managers, but are best evaluated by direct observation. This kind of feedback on actual output (use in business) is highly useful information for measuring success, as well as for determining where "consequence reinforcement" is needed to provide added motivation and where modeling and coaching would be beneficial.

2. **Measured Process:**

   - Worker-to-Worker Feedback
   - Manager-to-Worker Feedback
   - Worker-to-Manager Feedback

Those responsible for introducing the Language of Work into the business will want to pay special attention to its everyday use. They will need to encourage the use of the language between workers, managers and workers, and managers and managers. Modeling and coaching will help a great deal, but reinforcing the consequences for use of the work language should be encouraged. Encourage the workers and managers to let you know about their successes and where they need help. Provide them with feedback as they are learning and applying the language, not just at the end of the outputs they produce.

Once you have introduced the Language of Work in Phase 1 and have used it for six to nine months, the workers and managers will be ready to expand the application of the work language to the entire business and its various processes and work groups.

Phase 2: Expanding the Use of the Language of Work

Figure 7.2 is an implementation plan for Phase 2. In Phase 2 you will be expanding the application of the language to the Process, Work Group, and Business Unit levels of the Business Sphere. A description of each of the six elements of the implementation plan will give you a clear picture of what to do in the second phase. We begin with outputs.

Outputs of Phase 2

The major output is the utilization of the Language of Work on the Business Unit, Work Group, and Process levels. In Phase 2 the business will want to expand what the workers and managers have learned about their own work functions to those levels of the business that affect the business as a whole. The preferred order of application would be business unit, processes, individuals, and work groups. Note that even though the individuals have already, in Phase 1, begun to apply the language themselves, there will be a need to reassess individual applications in light of newly defined, subsequent Business Unit and Process Analysis. There is here a balance between the best way to initially learn the language—beginning at the Individual level—and the best sequence in which to apply the language—first the business unit, then processes, individuals, and finally work groups.

PHASE 2
IMPLEMENTATION PLAN
EXPANDING THE USE OF THE LANGUAGE OF WORK
(Processes, Work Groups, Business Unit)

INPUTS

Business Unit Needs
Process Needs
Work Group Needs
Work Application Tools

CONDITIONS

Performance Paradigm
Management Commitment

PROCESS

Workshop
Modeling
Coaching
Team Analysis

OUTPUT

Improved effectiveness and efficiency in:
- Business Unit
- Processes
- Work Groups

CONSEQUENCES

Expanded use at all levels of work:
- Improved effectiveness and efficiency of the entire business
  "Whole Boat Must Rise"
- Improved communications and morale
- "Super Glue"
- Profit

FEEDBACK

Measuring the output—Measured results
Measured process:
- Business Unit
- Processes
- Work Groups

Figure 7.2

177

Inputs for Phase 2

Once you know what the outputs are, your knowledge of the Language of Work tells you that the major inputs correspond to meeting the outputs. In Phase 2 this means that the major inputs are the business needs related to improving the business unit, processes, and work groups. A major aid in helping to define the needs in Phase 2 will be the work application tools—primarily the use of work diagrams and work relationship maps, combined with performance questions.

Conditions of Phase 2

Conditions in Phase 2 are the same as those in Phase 1. Analysis teams functioning to define the business unit, processes, and work groups will follow the Performance Paradigm—it is the primary condition. Again, as in Phase 1, management commitment is a primary condition.

Process for Phase 2

A workshop, modeling, and coaching combination of interventions is generally sufficient for introducing the application of the Language of Work to the business unit, processes, and work groups. We add to these a Team Analysis approach. Since the use of the workshop, modeling, and coaching was described in Phase 1 and these apply to Phase 2 in the same manner, a description of the Team Analysis approach is all that will be needed at this time.

Team analysis has been suggested throughout this book because it affords an efficient and effective way to achieve several goals. We know it is useful to involve everyone in the business as much as possible, but even this requires some efficient organization and processing to keep the analysis from lagging behind expectations and meaningful results. As described in Chapter 4, the analysis team is usually composed of both managers and workers representing a cross section of the business unit, work group, or process being analyzed. Equally important is that the team also has members who represent clients (customers) and suppliers to the business unit, process, or work group. In any analysis, we value the input of those who are affected by what we do—our clients—as well as those who influence what we will be doing—the suppliers. But, this is not the end of our need to involve others.

In Team Analysis we must take our analysis work (e.g., work diagram and performance questions) and have it reviewed by the broader audience of the business that the team represents. This means taking our analysis work diagrams and performance questions to the other managers and workers and asking for their input. In doing so, we hope to gain not only useful information for refining our definitions, but a commitment to what has been defined and will be measured. Without the commitment of the broader audience, we may well be doomed to failure, no matter how good our analysis is. Since in Phase 1 we have established a working knowledge of the Language of Work and a commitment to it by the work force in general, we can be somewhat assured that the involvement of the work force in Phase 2—should we encourage it—will be both welcomed and seen as positive by all workers and managers.

Consequences of Phase 2

There are primarily four consequences we hope to achieve in Phase 2:

1. Improved effectiveness and efficiency of the entire business

2. Improved communications and morale

3. Attainment of "Super Glue"

4. Increased profit

The consequences of Phase 2 relate to the use of the work language on all levels of the business and the combined effect this has on the entire business. The first consequence suggests that the work language has indeed been used on all four levels of the business, thus improving the effectiveness and efficiency of the entire business—the "whole boat has risen." The second consequence suggests that as a result of this, the communication and morale of the work force has improved. The work force knows more about the business than they did before and have participated in improving it in many ways. This usually increases morale.

The third consequence is a topic introduced at the end of Chapter 2. You will recall that many kinds of "business glues" are used to help hold a business together and move it forward. The Language of Work was described as an especially effective business glue—a super glue—in that it provides a way for the work force to fully understand the business and participate in its improvement. The involvement of the work force in using the Language of Work throughout the entire business in Phase 2 results in the attainment of the "super glue."

Finally, it would naturally follow that attainment of the above three consequences should result in increased profits for the business. This is usually a direct consequence, but it may be hidden. For example, a failing business that improves its effectiveness and efficiency may still be losing money, but less of it. If it has not increased profit, it has at least reduced its losses. The point is, the Language of Work does have a positive impact on the financial picture.

Feedback in Phase 2

As has been stated throughout this book, feedback has two primary aspects: One relates to feedback once the output is delivered (finished, complete), and the other is feedback as it relates to processing.

In Phase 2 we will provide information on the measurement of the overall impact of the Language of Work on producing the major business outputs. This includes results from the measurements of such consequences as overall customer satisfaction, profit/loss, employee satisfaction, and the like. These tell the work force, stockholders, board of directors, CEO, president, and others, that the business has benefited from the work language.

In measuring process, we look at the specific outputs for the processes, individuals, and work groups. These were described in Chapters 3 through 6. The results of the feedback tell us that the processes are well defined and work, that the individuals are skilled and meet their client needs, and that the work groups are organized in the right way to help the individuals and effectively aid in processing. If the results suggest otherwise, we know where to look to improve the process, individual, and work group.

There is no easy way to predict how long Phase 2 will take to achieve the desired consequences. As has been learned in various quality programs, it can take years and is a never-ending process. It can be anticipated that the Language of Work will help us get there quicker, with more understanding and outstanding results.

THE MAJOR CONSEQUENCES OF USING THE LANGUAGE OF WORK

There are, of course, a number of consequences that result from the use of the Language of Work. Many of these have been previously described as the benefits resulting from the application of the work language to the four levels of a business. Other consequences were described in reference to the work language in general. Here we focus on the two major consequences that result for the business as a whole—the consequences that make your business the ideal Business Sphere:

1. An informed work force

2. A quality-driven culture

The Informed Work Force

The Language of Work has an impact on managers and workers in significant ways. Both become, as I like to call it, "informed." They become the "informed manager" and the "informed worker."

The Informed Manager

The management-led approach to business has prevailed for a long time, and it still dominates the way business today approaches business operations and improvements. This means that management decides what will be improved, by whom, by when, with what, and whether or not measurement will be used to verify the results. Management also determines what major or minor role the individual worker will play in these improvements. An "informed manager" approach reforms the "management-led" approach into a more enlightened perspective, emphasizing what work really is and how it is best achieved and improved. In general terms, this means a cultural change for managers in how they perceive work and define, measure, improve, administer, and implement work. Thus, they become *"more* informed."

To be an informed manager, one must achieve fifteen standards, which are described on the following pages and listed separately in Figure 7.3.

---

15 Standards of the Informed Manager

1. Informed managers understand that work is accomplished through a process and not predominantly through the organizational structure.

2. Informed managers view outputs as what should be measured first, before any change is made in any other part of the Performance Paradigm.

3. Informed managers recognize that "getting work done" is not merely getting output finished but also doing what it takes to have workers perform work in the best way possible.

4. Informed managers involve others.

5. Informed managers recognize and develop talent.

6. Informed managers have the ability to handle conflict.

7. Informed managers facilitate work rather than do the work for the workers.

8. Informed managers "manage by walking around."

9. Informed managers listen and act on worker ideas.

10. Informed managers rotate workers.

11. Informed managers let go of control.

12. Informed managers promote an information-rich environment.

13. Informed managers "read the writing on the wall."

14. Informed managers do not resist change.

15. Informed managers push decision making down into the organization.

Figure 7.3

1. **Informed managers understand that work is accomplished through a process and not predominantly through the organizational structure.**

   Work is not simply a matter of taking some inputs and producing some outputs through some process; there are additional important elements of work, including conditions, consequences, and feedback. There is also the need to continually seek improved standards in the work. Managers who understand all six elements of the work language know how to get work accomplished through the proper facilitation of all elements of the work. In like manner, they also understand why workers cannot get certain work done on time, within budget, and to standards. And if managers approach the planning of work by learning why workers cannot get something done right the first time, they can then anticipate problems and plan how to help the workers do the work right the next time. Stated another way, managers who concentrate on only output and process do not fully know what "work" is; therefore, they do not know what it takes to make work better. These managers need to understand the entire Performance Paradigm.

   Managers must also understand that although work groups are the structure for organizing work, they are not the critical thing to change first *if they are to improve the business*. First, managers must define, analyze, and improve the processes through the Language of Work; then they can decide if a change in the work groups would help facilitate the efficient and effective use of the process.

2. **Informed managers view outputs as what should be measured first, before any change is made in any other part of the Performance Paradigm.**

   One of the oddest procedures to observe is that of managers changing processes before they have determined if there is anything wrong with the outputs. Most managers will claim they do measure outputs, when in fact they do not. True, they do have a general sense that something is wrong with an output, but ask them what measurement they have done beyond a mere guess or "feeling," with the internal or external client who received that output, and see what answer you receive. Having asked hundreds of managers to tell me what their outputs are, and having seen them take a long time to define these outputs (often mixing outputs with consequences), I can assure you that, despite any claims to the contrary, these managers have not measured outputs, for it is impossible to measure outputs without knowing precisely what the outputs are in the first place. An informed manager can tell you precisely what his or her outputs are, how he or she measures them, and exactly what clients think about them. Such managers are able to effectively communicate these to workers and facilitate the attainment of the outputs.

3. **Informed managers recognize that "getting work done" is not merely getting output finished but also doing what it takes to have workers perform work in the best way possible.**

How many times have you heard a manager say, "We haven't got time for training. We have to get the work done!" More recently, the excuse is "We haven't got time to deal with this total quality management stuff and do the work as well!" These managers need a change in perspective—need to become informed managers. Certainly, everyone understands timelines. But just how many managers believe that workers are fully skilled and qualified to do the work in the best way possible all the time? The more recent emphasis on "continuous improvement" is a step in the right direction. Informed managers are not just getting work done! They have realized that they also need to look continuously for ways to get it done better the next time. The Language of Work focuses attention on improving work continuously, not just now and then—or never.

4. **Informed managers involve others.**

Traditional management centers on the manager as a problem solver, whereas informed management recognizes the value of others as part of the process of problem solving and implementation. The difference is not just involving a greater number of people in the process; rather, it is largely a matter of recognizing that there are others who are part of the work process beyond those who immediately are doing the work under the direction of a given manager. Informed managers recognize that the inputs their workers use are the outputs from others. They also recognize that the outputs their workers produce are the inputs to others. Thus, there are suppliers (of inputs) and customers (using outputs) who can and should be asked to lend their perspective, evaluation, and general help in improving the total work process. Managers also need to pay attention to time and consequence factors between work groups, not only to getting work done within their own work groups. Defining and measuring work-group relationships, shared processes (SP), and overall processes (OP) will greatly help the manager involve others.

5. **Informed managers recognize and develop talent.**

Managers tend to rely on others (e.g., the training department) in the business to help in the development of their workers. This is all well and good as one resource, but informed managers take it upon themselves to identify worker development needs and provide training themselves in the form of coaching, mentoring, and good old-fashioned apprenticeship. Remember that businesses hire people for their capabilities and should allow them to use those capabilities. But also recognize that people need development either because they generally do lack some skills or because the business changes to meet new demands. Also, many workers want to improve their skills for their own professional development. Informed managers use the Language of Work, in the form of work plans and other application tools, to give complete and honest performance reviews, to plan for career development, and to measure individual and group performance for the sake of improving the processes for which they *and* the workers are ultimately responsible. Then informed managers follow through to develop talent, including their own.

6. **Informed managers have the ability to handle conflict.**

Conflict is as likely to occur in the Business Sphere as it is in our personal relationships. It may be buried in the Business Sphere a little bit deeper, but it does still exist. For the informed manager, it is a matter of identifying potential conflict, handling what conflict does occur, and being proactive in order to prevent it from occurring in the first place.

Two of the more common forms of conflict in business are those which arise from (1) the lack of clearly knowing one's own role, and (2) a breakdown in relationships between workers. The latter occurs in the chain of events where one worker hands off his or her output as an input to another worker. Workers are often heard to say, "If others would simply do their part, I could do mine!" This is a role-relationship conflict.

Informed managers can see the immediate benefit of the Language of Work as a basic communication means for all workers to describe not only their own work but also the processes they use, the work group they function within, the total business unit they are contributing to, and the work of others around them. The Language of Work is used to clarify roles, to work on relationships with other positions and processes, and to reduce conflict with management through clearer task assignments.

7. **Informed managers facilitate work rather than do the work for the workers.**

Managers usually come from the ranks of workers; therefore, they are used to "doing work." Often many of these former workers, now managers, continue to do the work of those under their direction. They do this partly out of necessity but mostly out of their belief that they know how to accomplish the work better than anyone else—otherwise, how did they get to be managers? These individuals need to gain a more useful perspective on their role as "manager." This role is more effective for the operation of the work group, implementation of the process, and overall working relationship. Informed managers realize that their job as a manager is to "facilitate."

Facilitators recognize that workers are hired for their capabilities, and if workers lack certain capabilities, it is the job of the manager to increase those capabilities to a satisfactory level. This relates to item five above, need to recognize the importance of developing the worker and not just concentrate on getting the work done. Thus, if workers are hired for their capability, they should be allowed to use that capability; the manager should not do the job for them. This is a recognition far easier for the worker to understand than for the typical manager to recognize and allow to occur. Informed managers use the Language of Work to facilitate work by (1) allowing workers to do *their own* work, (2) providing the necessary inputs for the work to be initiated, (3) clarifying what conditions must be adhered to, (4) supporting the process, (5) seeking and giving appropriate feedback during processing, (6) checking for standards regarding the output, and (7) at the conclusion of the output and during processing, reinforcing positive consequences. These are all elements of the Language of Work for improving the business. Any time the manager does the work, he or she reduces the time available to do any or all of these facilitating activities—the ones which truly define the manager.

8. Informed managers "manage by walking around."

Workers are familiar with the fact that the higher a manager rises in the organization, the less likely they are to see him or her. At best, such managers rush in and out of the work area as if they were late for their next appointment. Now, obviously, senior management has more and more responsibility and a wider field to observe. Be this as it may, it is extremely difficult to see work from an office or from a quick tour. The office is also a less than adequate place to ensure that workers do what they should be doing. Managing from an office is analogous to establishing policies and procedures: Once the manager, like a policy, is out of sight, he or she is usually ignored.

Informed managers get out and spend time with workers. Thus, they are ignored far less and are far more useful in observing and facilitating the work. Informed managers can judge what is happening in the workplace, because they enter the arena in which the elements of work occur. Here they are able to observe the inputs, see if the conditions are being adhered to and the process being used, provide feedback, check on output, and reinforce consequences. Equally important, the workers *see* and *talk* to managers who care about their work. Informed managers do not become informed by reading paperwork reports—they see the work for themselves or at least verify the contents of the paper in person.

9. **Informed managers listen and act on worker ideas.**

Workers have abundant ideas about how to do things better, faster, and in a less costly way. The problem is, managers do not always encourage such behavior; consequently, workers simply close up and do not make further suggestions. Why? Because nobody seems to care. Workers are often heard to say, "Managers are more concerned with getting the work done!" Informed managers know better. They know that any idea is worth considering, even if in the final analysis it has to be rejected for very sound reasons—at least the idea was presented and considered. There is always the possibility that an idea will be a real gem, and good ideas are worth waiting for, even if a manager must wade through a sea of other, minor ideas. Informed managers know that workers only present those ideas that have "perceived" merit, that they do this very infrequently, and that reviewing ideas is not time-consuming. But, if a manager is not open to new ideas, workers will not take the time to suggest *any* ideas—good or bad.

10. **Informed managers rotate workers.**

There is a perception in the workplace that one individual should be exclusively responsible for one job. Certainly, in the scheme of business, an individual has a particular job he or she does. But this does not mean that other individuals cannot be equipped to do someone else's job. The informed manager realizes that he or she needs to plan for contingencies. What if a person is out for a day, a week, a month, or even just a few hours? Why not have co-workers who can step in and help out? Will this cause insecurity in the person who is temporarily replaced? Only if the manager feeds that insecurity. The informed manager knows how to handle such feelings and is prepared with human resources that can be shifted to meet client demands and peak-work loads. The informed manager knows to plan for contingencies and to determine where they are needed.

11. **Informed managers let go of control.**

One manager I know admits to being a control freak. The truth is, many managers *are* control freaks. They are afraid to delegate any responsibility because they think something will go wrong. With such an attitude, according to Murphy's law, something surely will go wrong. As in personal life, control is an issue that destroys people. In business, the destruction is much more subtle: Workers smile but do not suggest ideas, ask for help, or in general communicate with managers who exercise control; instead, they go about their work in a protective mode and "quiet down" to a level that protects them from the control. Many go one step further and blame themselves or others. Managers who are informed and confident of their own ability do not need to exert control, because they facilitate the work force rather than manage in hard and fast ways.

12. Informed managers promote an information-rich environment.

One of the more common ways that businesses and their managers exercise control over workers is by manipulating information. Depending on the situation, they may either withhold information or misuse it. When information is withheld, workers are kept in the dark about the current status of a business or projected changes in the workplace, or they are denied constructive feedback. In its most frequent misuse, management employs statistical and financial information to support its "battle cry" for increased worker effort on an output. Rather than analyzing the problem at hand, encouraging worker cooperation, and providing positive consequences for achievements made, management uses sliding goals and resorts to pressuring the work force to meet those goals.

13. Informed managers "read the writing on the wall."

I once heard a fascinating story about an executive who took a unique approach to obtaining worker feedback on his company: He put butcher paper up on the walls in various work areas throughout the business and told people—workers at all levels—to write whatever they pleased on it. Similar to graffiti, the comments he received gave him a great deal of insight into those who wrote them, as well as all kinds of useful information on the culture of the business. He discovered what irritated workers, how they felt about managers, and where their dreams were not coming true. And, so the story goes, he started to do something about these problems.

Informed managers also "read the writing on the wall," although usually in a figurative, rather than a literal, sense. They must seek out this information and listen. They have to walk and see. In doing so, they have to know what to look for. If, for example, they only look for results information, they are missing not only customer satisfaction but opportunities for worker satisfaction and improving the processes. In like manner, if they are not seeking and giving feedback, they are not getting the information they need, and certainly the worker is not getting what he or she needs. The more familiar the manager is with the Language of Work, the more he or she knows what to look for.

14. Informed managers do not resist change.

One of most useful lessons I learned from my advisor in graduate school was this: Change brings conflict. Change is necessary if we are to grow, and therefore change is okay. Through many years of designing and implementing performance improvement programs and processes, I have naturally assumed the role of a change agent. For me, the realization that change was necessary and acceptable freed me to make continuous improvements *and* take risks. I have generally noted in business, however, that managers resist change because they perceive it as "rocking the boat." To carry the analogy used in this book one step further, they not only don't rock the boat, they don't make the boat rise to greater levels of effectiveness and efficiency. They build a set of sandbag levies around their work and manage those levies. They only change when the flood waters of crisis are lapping at their projects, reports, and other assorted outputs.

Informed managers realize that change is the way they can improve situations for themselves, for those who work with them, and thus for the business as a whole. To do this, they have to know what to change and how to change it; then they must involve others in the implementation of these changes, rather than impose change on others. This is best done by using the Language of Work as it applies to the four levels of the Business Sphere.

15. **Informed managers push decision making down into the organization.**

Of the following alternatives, which would you prefer? Would you rather make a decision yourself and follow through on it, or would you feel more comfortable if someone else made the decision for you and you only had to follow through on it? The former is preferred by most people. Why? Because you immediately have ownership and an investment in the eventual solution by making the decision yourself. Of course, not all decisions can be made by workers, but when and where possible it is best to push the decision making down into the organization. Many businesses have started doing this and have found that the lower-echelon worker not only willingly takes on the added responsibility but seriously executes it with due care and caution. More importantly, the customers or clients he or she serves appreciate the quick response to their needs. Delayed responses, after all, do irritate customers and clients, be they internal or external customers and clients.

Informed managers know how to push decision making down into the organization by helping workers become the ones best able to solve problems in conjunction with their suppliers (those who make an input) and their clients (those who receive their work). Furthermore, they put workers in this position by also encouraging them to suggest improvements in the business. By using the Language of Work to understand their jobs, workers are able to scan the environment of the entire business, make suggestions, and become involved in solutions for the entire business.

These 15 standards do not cover everything that an informed manager is or does, but they are highly representative of what it takes to have an informed management.

Informed Workers

Early in this book, I stated that the greatest gains in business improvement were realized when individual workers made performance improvements through their own efforts. The Language of Work can be the way for individual workers to achieve this end. When the workers become informed, they can make their own improvements.

To be an informed worker, one must achieve twelve standards, which are described on the following pages and listed separately in Figure 7.4.

---

12 Standards of the Informed Worker

1. Informed workers know their jobs.

2, Informed workers measure client satisfaction.

3. Informed workers pursue self-improvement.

4. Informed workers seek help.

5. Informed workers develop their careers.

6. Informed workers ask for feedback.

7. Informed workers look for improved relationships with others.

8. Informed workers actively secure their inputs rather than wait for others to deliver them (as outputs).

9. Informed workers have a positive relationship with management.

10. Informed workers use influence to make difficult changes happen.

11. Informed workers know where they fit into the business and largely contribute to the business by understanding it.

12. Informed workers feel good about their work.

Figure 7.4

1. **Informed workers know their jobs.**

An individual's job comprises more than the specific tasks the individual carries out as work. Although most workers can roughly tell others in the business what they do, can they communicate this information fully and clearly, using some common work language? If they could, there would be greater understanding and cooperation between workers. The trouble is, businesses lack a common work language that the entire work force (or even a fraction of it) knows and uses.

Informed workers understand every facet of their jobs, from what they begin with as inputs to the process they will use, including how inputs and process are influenced by existing conditions. Furthermore, informed workers know the standards that the output must achieve, and they attempt to meet those standards on a consistent basis. They realize the consequences of their work both for the business and themselves, and not only encourage feedback but actively seek it out, ensuring for themselves that outputs and performance are at an optimum level. Informed workers communicate with their clients to make sure they are satisfied, and if the clients are not, these workers accept the opportunity and challenge to reach client satisfaction by making the necessary changes to their work. They want to achieve more than client satisfaction, for they know that exceeding it will result in a client returning for new business. Informed workers are able to accomplish these things because they can define their jobs, measure them, and communicate them to any other individual in the business in terms of inputs, conditions, process, outputs, consequences, and feedback.

2. **Informed workers measure client satisfaction.**

Does the average worker ask for an evaluation from his or her clients as to their satisfaction with the output the worker has given them? Such proactive behavior is rare. By contrast, informed workers seek such information from their clients not only to find out how well they have done a job, but also to determine how they can do the job better. Informed workers have defined their jobs, know what to measure, and personally go to clients and measure satisfaction on their own. They do this to be the best that they can be.

3. **Informed workers pursue self-improvement.**

No job is stagnant; things change and new ways to make improvement are developed. A worker can either sit back and assume the business will do what it takes to keep workers up to date and to improve their performance, or the worker can take the initiative. Most businesses try their best to assure improvements are made. Individuals could do more if they knew how. The Language of Work can show them how. It can be used to help them identify where inputs need to be made better, where to improve the process, what conditions to pay attention to, what the expected outputs are, what consequences to expect, and where and when to seek feedback. Informed workers go to other skilled workers and their management and discuss their own performance improvement needs. They work out plans for the attainment of these improved skills.

4. Informed workers seek help.

All workers need help at some time or another, if not daily, then weekly. There are many needs that can trigger this search for help. Perhaps a worker has insufficient tools for completing a task or does not understand some nuance of the process. The elementary question is, "What do workers do about seeking help?" Sad as it is, the average worker does not seek help until a problem occurs. Seeking help at the time of a problem is usually a stress-related event in which a manager or another worker is thinking, "Why didn't this person come to me earlier?" and the worker is thinking, "Why didn't I do something about this earlier?" The truth of the matter is, most of us don't like to admit we need help, and the workplace environment traditionally has been less than conducive for seeking help. The environment can be changed, however, and opportunities for openness established.

Informed workers know that seeking out help is a matter of doing business in both an effective and efficient way. When viewed as a necessary part of seeking and asking for feedback within the performance of work, help is but a necessary function in business, as are the needed inputs, process, conditions to be followed, and consequences that will occur. Informed workers realize this and seek help whenever a level of uncertainty occurs.

5. Informed workers develop their careers.

It was not so true a few years ago, but now few people in business stay in the same job for any extended length of time. Job security is virtually gone. Some workers will change their job focus as much as five or more times throughout their working life. Few workers will continue doing the same job for several years. Today's businesses are much more dynamic and subject to shifting market trends. Of course, businesses are planning for change with or without the participation of workers and many managers. In today's business, workers cannot assume the business will plan for their welfare. Workers and managers are smart to anticipate and prepare for change in business. The saying "The early bird gets the worm" will apply more than ever before. Besides, who better to plan and be in charge of *your* career than yourself!

191

Informed workers develop their careers through seeking other employment within or outside the business they work for. Informed workers may look for career opportunities, but the wise ones prepare while doing their current jobs. The Language of Work provides a convenient way for the informed worker to know what others are doing, what it takes to do it, and what consequences are likely to occur. With such information in hand, the informed worker identifies new outputs (job responsibilities) and seeks the cooperation of management and other workers to learn them. The worker who sits back and waits for management to do this kind of planning may well wait a long time. In addition, informed workers prepare for other job accountabilities that make them more valuable to the business in times of special need.

6. **Informed workers ask for feedback.**

Most workers tend to wait for others to tell them whether they are doing things right or to seek confirmation of a job well done. This tendency may be rooted in a reluctance to appear eager for praise or in the fear that others will interpret this as a sign of inadequacy. Informed workers, however, realize that feedback is a basic part of work, that it is needed to determine whether things have gone right, and that feedback makes them feel good. Confident people pursue feedback on a continuous basis, feeling they deserve nothing less. If managers are hesitant or forget to give feedback, workers need to seek it all that much more on their own.

7. **Informed workers look for improved relationships with others.**

Placing blame on others is as common in business life as in personal life, if not more so. We know that much improvement in business could be realized if workers would only seek ways to work more closely with other workers—particularly those in different work groups. Informed workers use the Language of Work in the Business Sphere to know exactly who their clients and input suppliers are. Then, they seek ways to improve communication and meet one another's expectations and schedules. Informed workers know that their output is someone else's input, and so they try to improve anything that will make their mutual relationship effective and efficient.

8. **Informed workers actively secure their inputs rather than wait for others to deliver them (as outputs).**

On the surface this may seem like a minor point, but it has significant implications for business. Typically, workers are used to completing their tasks and delivering their outputs to internal or external clients when *the workers* think the outputs are ready. Thus, the client is left to wait until the worker decides to deliver—unless he or she puts pressure on the worker. The client is, in a sense, at the worker's mercy. Also, the worker can deliver the client's output without following up for feedback on what was delivered. This is similar to giving classroom instruction without asking the students if they liked or used the content. Informed workers reverse the order—they go and get the inputs, actively securing them. What this means is that they not only can make contact with the suppliers, but they can have some say about whether they need clarity on the inputs. They can also ask any necessary questions and, in general, assure that the inputs meet their requirements.

9. **Informed workers have a positive relationship with management.**

Too often adversarial relationships develop between workers and management. When there are problems, this "us and them" point of view fixes blame or shifts it, depending on the situation, but does not help anyone arrive at a solution. This is not to say that when workers are informed there will be no conflicts, because there are parts of the business that management controls—from schedules to compensation—and they will not always be satisfying to workers. But informed workers realize that there are ways to work with management to get work done in the most effective and efficient manner. The Language of Work, through its focus on the Business Sphere, provides a way for workers to see what is going on in the business and for managers to communicate more clearly the reasoning behind their decisions. Informed workers, in turn, use the Language of Work to respond to management or to discuss further issues.

10. **Informed workers use influence to make difficult changes happen.**

Workers and managers are inclined to think that only those in high positions of authority can get business problems resolved, especially when it comes to how the business will change itself to make improvements and who will be responsible for those changes. In the eyes of workers, only management has the power and authority to effect change. However, the informed worker realizes that there is another way to bring about change. It's called influence.

Influence, by definition, is swaying a person's thoughts so that he or she will behave in a certain way without being forced to. And there are many ways to influence someone. For example, informed workers know that when they want a change to occur, they should involve management in devising, deriving, and implementing the solution and measuring its effectiveness. If a manager does not want to get involved, an informed worker will at least keep the manager abreast of the situation. In these ways, the manager has a vested interest in the solution and can use his or her authority, power, or *influence* with others to get the solution accepted. But informed workers also know that an information-rich environment is also a key to influence. Workers who inform managers tend to have greater influence in the business.

11. Informed workers know where they fit into the business and largely contribute to the business by understanding it.

Unless the business is a very small concern, it is more than likely that most workers know relatively little about the business they work in. They show up for work, do what they do, and go home. Yes, they may know their own department and those around them, but what knowledge and appreciation do they have for what others are doing? If there were more understanding, would the problems associated with handing off lower-quality work to others occur as often as it does? Would outputs be as late as they sometimes are?

The Language of Work provides a frame of reference for understanding a business from inside to outside—the entire Business Sphere. Workers and managers alike can understand work diagrams for the entire business unit, work groups, processes, and their own and others' jobs. The Language of Work promotes an information-rich work environment, and being informed through information helps build everything from cooperation to quality.

12. Informed workers feel good about their work.

Have you ever talked to a worker who just loves his or her job? Do you know of a company where there are lots of these people and the business is doing well? If so, then what is the key to such success? Is it the working conditions, the pay, the nature of the work itself? Of course, the answer is all of these and many other factors as well.

Underlying a person's good feeling about work is the knowledge that "I am valued." And while the basis of this comes from knowing and feeling good about oneself to begin with, informed workers seek out businesses and ways of operating in those businesses that promote understanding, participation, positive feedback, open communication, sharing ideas, growth, and fun. Businesses that value workers provide workers with the means and opportunity to understand and participate in the business—not just work in it.

To meet the standards of informed individuals, both workers and managers must come to understand and apply a new way of doing business. They need to take on the Language of Work as a means for understanding, communicating, applying, and measuring business. When they do, these become a way of life and the Language of Work infuses and improves their "work culture"—the final consequence and concluding thought to be described in this book.

A Quality-Driven Culture

A major emphasis in today's business is quality—quality as a method designed to improve client satisfaction and therefore profitability. Businesses aim to have what is commonly referred to as a quality-driven culture—the ongoing, everyday attention paid by workers and managers to assure that internal and external clients receive products that possess the best quality possible. How does a business become driven by quality? What prevents business from being quality-driven? Of course, many factors are involved. The total quality management movement has made many inroads, but the goal of a consistent quality culture has eluded most organizations. I believe the most fundamental part of the failure to achieve a quality-driven culture lies in the absence of a useful, universal work language for the work force. A look at a comprehensive definition of culture will reveal what it takes to build a quality-driven culture. We can then see how the Language of Work is a major contributor to, if indeed not the very foundation of, building a truly quality-driven culture—this will be a major consequence of the Language of Work.

. Culture is defined in many ways, but *Merriam-Webster's Collegiate Dictionary* offers an especially functional definition, appropriate to seeing the value of a universal work language in the workplace.

> *Culture is the integrated pattern of human behavior that includes* ***thought, speech, action, and artifacts*** *and depends upon man's capacity for learning and transmitting knowledge to succeeding generations.*

You can see in the definition that culture includes four major items:

- Thought

- Speech

- Action

- Artifacts

We will look at each of these items (summarized in Figure 7.5, on the following page) in terms of (1) traditional business practices, (2) the impact that TQM and other continuous improvement processes have had on fostering a quality culture, and (3) where the Language of Work provides the missing link that bridges the gap to a truly *quality-driven* culture.

COMPARATIVE BUSINESS CULTURES

	TRADITIONAL BUSINESS	IMPACT OF TQM	THE LANGUAGE OF WORK
THOUGHT	• Management says/ Workers do	• Mission Statement	✓ Expanded view of work ✓ One language fits all ✓ Paradigm shift: Quality Is Me
ACTION	• Manager tells/ Worker does	• Empower the worker • Emphasize measurement • Process driven	✓ Single model application tools ✓ View all of business with one model ✓ Analytical way of thinking and acting ✓ Intuitive action
ARTIFACTS	• Output variable • Profit centered	• Consistent output • Increased client satisfaction	✓ Greater client satisfaction ✓ Quality-driven output
SPEECH	• Technical Languages • Financial Language	• Suppliers • Customers • Measurement	✓ Can communicate about own job, processes, work groups, and business unit—the entire Business Sphere

Figure 7.5

Thought

1. Traditional Business

Traditionally, *thought* in most businesses has been management-domi-nated. Management decided what was to be produced, under what condi-tions, when, with what, and how. It was not unusual that the prevailing attitude was "So what if the worker doesn't like what is to be done? It will be done as we, the management, say it will be." Workers' feelings and needs were considered unimportant; those that were important could not be acted upon because the business did not functionally know how to act on them. If the business were to be changed, management would do it. Management made reorganization the weapon of choice for change. In many businesses, the work force could look forward to being reorganized to *improve work* (change the culture) as many as eight times over a ten-year span. A new alignment of departments and resources, or a new head of operations, would solve the problem—would "change the culture." The outcome, however, was that reorganization did not always change business in a positive way; all it did was force people to look for new alliances to provide a more secure setting for their individual insecurity. The culture may have appeared to change, but rarely was the change for the better.

2. Impact of TQM

TQM brought into the business world the need to give careful attention and commitment to thought. This occurred through a process of defining quality and basing the company's efforts to achieve quality on mission statements. According to the stated mission, both management and worker would cooperatively agree to move forward to achieve client satisfaction. Thus, businesses began defining and ensuring that everyone in the busi-ness understood its mission as a business. These statements of mission began to appear at the entrance to every building, in publications of the business, and in reference to all kinds of activities. The mission statement was intended to provide a guiding light and a benchmark against which to measure action. However, in the same way that the conditions of work are only as good as the actions to fulfill them, thought, while necessary and important, is itself only as good as the action taken by managers and workers to reflect that thought.

3. The Language of Work

The Language of Work contributes to the thought of a culture in three unique ways. First, it fosters an expanded view of work and what it takes to achieve the mission. The business is able to more accurately and com-pletely define the business (business unit, process, work groups, and individuals) that will be necessary to achieve its mission—its thought. Its thought is a clear sense of what work truly is and how to achieve work effectively and efficiently.

Second, the Language of Work promotes a thought process of "One Language Fits All." Managers and workers use the six elements of the work language, through various application tools, to analyze, improve, implement, and administer work as a single thought process, rather than use the more random, multimodel approach of traditional business or even the multiprocess models of TQM.

Finally, the Language of Work provides a paradigm shift to self-action and responsibility for what the managers and workers do. This thought shows the individual worker how to effect improvements in work on their own. The shift is to "Quality Is Me."

Action

1. Traditional Business

The short version of *action* in business has traditionally taken the form of managers telling workers what work to do and workers doing the work. Management had the attitude that workers only needed to do what they were told and follow the procedures that had been established. The consequence was that workers got used to saying nothing to improve the business, because management was not interested in hearing what they felt they already knew.

2. The Impact of TQM

Total Quality Management altered business' view of *action* by introducing the idea of *empowering* the work force. This meant getting the worker involved in improving quality. It meant involving the clients and suppliers. This change in action changed the culture of many businesses. The culture manifests itself in action through all kinds of worker-driven involvement, reliance on measurement, and increased training—all of which are consistent with the definition of a culture. Some of the tools and actions of TQM do involve everyone (such as ad hoc and permanent process improvement teams), and when results are achieved, everyone participates in "celebration" events. However, many of the tools and actions are less worker-driven (initiated and used by the worker) than they are process-driven (a procedural way of doing things). Process-driven procedures include re-engineering, fast cycle time, "value-added" procedures, and so forth. While these process-driven tools for actions contribute to an increasingly quality-driven culture, and are certainly far better than management-led attempts at quality (often dominated by only the quality assurance and quality control units), something is still missing to make the culture truly quality-driven.

3. The Language of Work

The Language of Work provides a new set of tools for *action*, ones that are based on a single model rather than on a multiplicity of procedures and methodologies. We call these work application tools. These are across-the-board, universal tools that individuals can use on their own and with others, and on the processes, in work groups, and in the business unit. The work application tools that have been described and illustrated in this book are powerful means to action. They provide a way to define and measure the whole of the business so that everyone understands the business better. The work force has, in the Language of Work, a way to view business as a systematic process; they have an analytical way of thinking and acting, transcending the more traditional view of business or TQM as a set of procedures to follow. Unlike TQM with its memorized formulas for action, the Language of Work, as any language of communication, becomes *intuitive* through long-term use. Thus, the actions of workers and managers become highly analytical, systematic, and client-centered—actions that represent a quality-driven culture.

Artifacts

The artifacts of culture are the results that are produced by a culture.

1. Traditional Business

In traditional business, the emphasis has been on profit and the volume of output, which is variable because of changing environmental conditions. Typically, not enough attention was paid to the client, and in many cases, eventually the output was no longer valued by the client, allowing competition to replace the business or at least some of its market share.

2. The Impact of TQM

TQM brought greater attention to the client and thus increased client satisfaction. The consequence of this change has generally been better and more consistently produced artifacts.

3. The Language of Work

The Language of Work provides tools that are easy to understand and apply, facilitates a better understanding of the business, and encourages more direct involvement of the individual. The result is better artifacts—that is, there is more quality to the outputs and greater client satisfaction.

Speech

We come to the fourth and final element of culture—the one to which the Language of Work contributes in a singularly significant way.

1. Traditional Business

The introduction to this book described a missing basic ingredient in business: a method for *talking about work*—a way for workers to talk to workers, workers to talk to managers, managers to talk to workers, and managers to talk to other managers. Traditional business has always fallen short in a common work language. It has relied instead on technical and financial languages.

2. The Impact of TQM

TQM has introduced new tools and some vocabulary, but no work language. It has provided *speech* in which the work force addresses the needs of suppliers and customers. It has also provided ways to act and talk in terms of measuring for needed improvements and measuring client satisfaction. Still, there is no way to talk work.

3. The Language of Work

The Language of Work provides the *speech* of culture, which results in new and systematic *thought, action,* and improved *artifacts.*

The overriding major consequences of the new Language of Work—understood and spoken by everyone in the business—is that it helps individuals understand fully their own work, how to improve it themselves, and how to measure their clients' satisfaction. The Language of Work helps everyone in a business share an understanding of work with everyone else in the business; *everyone* understands and knows how to make improvements intuitively as well as procedurally. Just as we learn the language we speak and it becomes automatic to us, so too can the Language of Work become second nature to us and be in our everyday thoughts as we *intuitively* drive quality in our businesses. Expecting a work force to build a quality-driven culture without a common work language is like expecting two nations speaking different languages to appreciate the fact that, whereas one of them enjoys eating meat, the other is vegetarian because it reveres all living things as sacred. A total quality-driven culture can never be fully achieved without a common work language spoken and used by everyone in the culture.

As a closing thought, it is hard to imagine being able to "walk the talk" unless one is fully capable of being able to "talk" work in the first place. Alfred Korzybski (1958), the noted mid-20th-century Polish-born scientist and philosopher who studied the continuity of culture, tells us that the *first* and *primary* means of culture transmission is, not surprisingly, the *language* of a society. We know that businesses have their own society within them. As long as businesses lack a common work language, we must question if a true quality-driven culture can flourish at all. This question is corroborated by analyzing, as we have, the definition of culture. As you move forward with the newfound position, perspective, and understanding of work you have learned in this book—and having become the informed worker or informed manager—you can be assured that your new Business Sphere, through the Language of Work, will truly achieve a quality-driven culture.

BIBLIOGRAPHY

Korzybski, Alfred. (1958). *Science and Sanity*. Lakeville, CT: International Non-Aristotelian Library Publishing Company.

Langdon, Danny G. (1991, August). Performance technology in three paradigms, *Performance & Instruction Journal*.

Langdon, Danny G., & Kathleen Whiteside. (1991). *The Performance Technology Workshop*. Santa Monica, CA: Performance International.

Rummler, Geary, & Alan P. Brache. (1991). *Improving Performance: How to Manage the White Space on the Organization Chart*. San Francisco: Jossey-Bass Publishers, Inc.

Stolovitch, Harold, & Erica Keeps. (1992). *The Handbook of Human Performance Technology*. San Francisco: Jossey-Bass Publishers, Inc.

INDEX